D0802146

Bible Commentary
NEW TESTAMENT

NELSON'S
POCKET
REFERENCE
SERIES

Bible Commentary
NEW TESTAMENT

THOMAS NELSON PUBLISHERS
Nashville

Published in Nashville, Tennessee, by Thomas Nelson, Inc.

The Bible version used in this publication is THE NEW KING JAMES VERSION. Copyright © 1979, 1980, 1982, Thomas Nelson, Inc., Publishers.

Printed in the United States of America.

7 — 04

Library of Congress Cataloging-in-Publication Data

Wiersbe, Warren W.
  Nelson's pocket reference Bible: New Testament commentary / Warren W. Wiersbe.
    p.   cm.
  Includes bibliographical references.
  ISBN 0-7852-4268-6
  1. Bible. N.T.—Commentaries. I. Title: Pocket reference Bible.
II. Thomas Nelson Publishers. III. Title.
BS2341.2.W542 2000
225.7—dc21   99–054027
                                                     CIP

Contents

Getting the Most Out of This Book

Nelson's *Pocket Reference Bible New Testament Commentary* is designed to be a supplement to your Bible and not a substitute for it. Its main purpose is to assist you in discovering and applying some of the basic spiritual lessons found in Scripture. Where needed, explanations of difficult texts are given, but this is not an "explanatory commentary" as such.

The Bible is God's truth (John 17:17), and that truth is given on several "levels." The foundation is *historical truth,* the record of facts and words that involve real people and real events. From these facts we learn *doctrinal truth* concerning God, man, sin, salvation, and a host of other subjects. Of course, the end result must be *practical truth,* for we get God's blessing by *doing* His Word and not simply by *learning* it (James 1:22–25). Learning must lead to living.

The Bible was written for the heart as well as for the mind and the will, which is where *devotional truth* comes in. We use the Bible devotionally when we allow it to speak to us personally as we are taught by the Spirit of God (John 14:26; 15:26; 16:13–15). All Scripture was not written *to* us, but it was written *for* us (2 Tim. 3:16–17); and it can enlighten, enable, enrich, and encourage us if we will only let it.

Charles Haddon Spurgeon, the famous British preacher, said, "No Scripture is of private interpretation: no text has spent itself upon the person who first received it. God's comforts are like wells, which no one man or set of men can drain dry, however mightily may be their thirst."

When we read the Bible devotionally, we focus on the spiritual essentials, not the historical or geographical accidentals. God has often encouraged me from the first chapter of Joshua, but this does not mean I can walk into the Jordan River and expect it to open up before me. However, I have

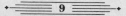

seen Him "open up" difficult situations in ministry as I have trusted Him.

The Word of God is given to warn us (1 Cor. 10:1–12) and to offer hope to us (Rom. 15:4). It can do these things for us only if we receive the Word personally and let it work in our lives (1 Thess. 2:13).

Christian biography is filled with examples of God's "speaking" to His servants from the Word and giving them just the truth they needed for making hard decisions or facing difficult challenges. My wife and I have experienced this in our ministry. God has revealed His mind to us at just the right time through a portion of Scripture that was a part of our regular daily reading. People who "just open the Bible anywhere" and ask for help are turning God's Word into a magic book and are tempting God, not trusting Him.

A word of caution here: we must be very careful of saying, "God told me to do this." God does not address us today as He did Moses and Joshua and Paul. It is far better to say, "This is what the Spirit revealed to me from the Word, and I'm praying about what God wants me to do." After all, Satan also knows how to use the Bible (Matt. 4:5–7). "It is written" must be balanced by "*Again* it is written."

If you want to get the most out of this book, I suggest that you do the following:

1. Have a program for reading the Bible, a definite time and place and a schedule to follow. Random Bible reading is better than no reading at all, but it is rarely edifying.

2. Read the passage carefully, asking the Spirit to instruct you. Meditate on it, and seek the truths God has for you. You may want to write down in a devotional journal what you discover in the Word.

3. Read the comments in the *New Testament Bible Commentary*, think about them, and assimilate whatever truths God impresses on your heart. Trace the cross-references; compare Scripture with Scripture, and see how one passage sheds light on another.

4. Pray the truth into your inner being, and ask the Spirit to help you put it into practice. True Bible knowledge, properly assimilated, will lead to a "burning heart" that wants to obey (Luke 24:32) and not to a "big head" that wants to show off (1 Cor. 8:1).

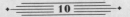

To benefit from this book, you do not have to agree with everything I have written. My comments on the Word are not the meal; they are the menu that describes the meal. They are not the road but signal lights that help point the way. If this book ever takes the place of your Bible, or of your own meditation on the Bible, you will cease to grow. Bible knowledge alone is not spiritual nutrition.

I have been reading the Bible faithfully ever since I became a Christian in 1945. Many comments in this book have come from material that I wrote in notebooks I have kept for the past twenty years. When my good friend and editor, Dr. Victor Oliver, suggested that I write a devotional commentary, I had the opportunity to examine those notebooks again and "mine" from them the truths that I thought would help fellow pilgrims on the path of life. At least they have helped me, and for this, I am grateful to the Lord.

WARREN W. WIERSBE

THE FOUR GOSPELS

◆

The word *gospel* means "good news." It is the message that Jesus Christ forgives the sins of all who trust in Him (1 Cor. 15:1–11; Gal. 1:6–9). *Gospel* also refers to the first four books of the New Testament, which present the life and teachings of the Savior. Apart from Jesus Christ—who He is, what He taught, and what He did—there can be no good news for lost sinners (Acts 4:12).

The four Gospels are not biographies in the modern sense of the word nor do they tell us everything about Jesus (John 20:30–31). Led by the Spirit, the authors selected material that helped them accomplish their purpose for writing.

Matthew wrote primarily for the Jews and explained that Jesus Christ is the Messiah who fulfills the Old Testament prophecies. Mark directed his book to the Romans and pictured Jesus as the active Servant of the Lord. Luke wrote for the Greeks and presented Jesus as the perfect and compassionate Son of man. John had the whole world in mind when he wrote and presented Jesus as Son of God and Savior of the world.

The first three Gospels give a somewhat parallel account of the life of Jesus and therefore are called "synoptic Gospels." (The word *synoptic* means "to see together.") John's gospel, written much later, contains material that supplements the accounts by the synoptic writers. Each gospel is unique, and all four are needed to provide a well-rounded view of the life, teachings, and works of Jesus Christ.

MATTHEW

◆

Matthew ("gift of God") was a Jewish tax collector who obeyed Christ's call and became one of the original twelve apostles (Matt. 9:9-13). His given name was Levi (Luke 5:27).

Writing especially for the Jews, Matthew proves that Jesus Christ is the Son of David, the Messiah, the rightful heir to David's throne. At least 129 Old Testament quotations and allusions appear in his gospel, and the word *kingdom* is found over fifty times. Matthew's gospel stands first in the New Testament as the perfect bridge between the old covenant and the new, Israel and the church, prophecy and fulfillment.

The King presented Himself to His people (chaps. 1—10), but the religious leaders resisted Him (chaps. 11—13). The King therefore withdrew from the crowds with His disciples to prepare them for His coming arrest and crucifixion (chaps. 14—20). He was rejected and crucified (chaps. 21—27), but He arose from the dead and commissioned His disciples to take His message to the whole world (chap. 28).

As you read Matthew's gospel, you will be impressed with the authority of Jesus Christ over disease, demons, circumstances, and even death. He has authority over our lives, and we should follow Him in obedience.

MATTHEW 1

A special book (1). The Old Testament is "the book of the genealogy of Adam" (Gen. 5:1), but the New Testament is "the book of the genealogy of Jesus Christ." In fact, the genealogy of Jesus Christ is the last one given in the Bible, here and in Luke 3:23-28. The important thing is not your *first* birth but your *second* birth (John 3).

A special providence (2-17). What may be to some readers

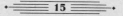

a boring list of difficult names is actually the record of God's working throughout the ages to bring His Son to earth. God ruled and overruled and fulfilled His great promises. In the same way, He will keep His promises and send Jesus back again.

A special Child (18–25). The birth of Jesus was different from every other birth: He was conceived by the Spirit in Mary's womb and born with a sinless nature. He is "God with us," and He is also God *like us* because He took our nature and entered into human life and experience. What a wonderful Savior!

The Virgin Birth	*The virgin birth of Jesus Christ is vital to the truth of the gospel (Isa. 7:14). Since Jesus Christ is God, He existed before Mary; therefore, He could not have been conceived as are other babies. He was not only born, but He "came into the world" (John 18:37). He is both God and man, the sinless Lamb of God (1 Pet. 1:19). Matthew opens and closes his book with "God with us" (1:23; 28:20).*

MATTHEW 2

What were the responses to His birth?

Creation responded by putting a miraculous star in the heavens to tell the world a King had been born (Num. 24:17).

The Gentiles responded by worshiping Him and bringing Him gifts. Matthew shows early in his book that Jesus came to save Gentiles as well as Jews. The wise men were astrologer-scientists who studied the heavens. The star led them to the Scriptures, and the Scriptures led them to the Savior. (See Ps. 19.) God speaks to us in ways we can understand.

Herod responded with fear and deception. He wanted no new King to threaten his reign.

The chief priests and scribes gave the right information but the wrong response. They were only five miles away from the Messiah, yet they refused to go to see Him! What good is it to understand Bible prophecy if it doesn't make a difference in your life?

The Magi The wise men (Magi) were scientists, yet they saw no conflict between science and Scripture or between searching for truth and worshiping the Savior. Devout Christians can worship the Lord with the mind as well as the heart (Matt. 22:37). "Science without religion is lame," said Albert Einstein. "Religion without science is blind."

MATTHEW 3

John the Baptist was a model preacher. He was a *road builder* who prepared the way for the Lord (v. 3; Isa. 40:3), and an *axman* who got to the root of sin and exposed it (v. 10). He was not intimidated by people, nor was he afraid to preach about judgment (v. 12). He was obedient to his Lord and magnified Him in all things (John 3:30).

Some people heard God's Word and confessed their sins (vv. 5–6), while others heard it and covered their sins (vv. 7–9; Prov. 28:13). The first group became children of God, but the second group were children of the devil (v. 7; John 8:44).

Jesus is the Son of God. The Scriptures (v. 3), John the Baptist (v. 11), the Holy Spirit (v. 16), and the Father (v. 17) attested to that truth.

Significance of Baptism

Jesus was not baptized to confess any sins (v. 5), since He was sinless. His baptism was His presentation to Israel (John 1:31) as well as a picture of His future baptism on the cross when "all the waves and billows" of judgment would go over Him (Matt. 20:22; Ps. 42:7). The baptism of John looked forward to the coming of Messiah (Acts 19:1–7). Christian baptism today looks back to the death, burial, and resurrection of Jesus Christ and witnesses of the believer's identification with Him (Col. 2:12; Acts 10:47–48).

MATTHEW 4

The Victor (1–11). Public ministry is built on private victory. Our Lord was not tempted so that God could examine Him, for the Father had already approved Him (3:17). He was tempted for our sake, that He might personally know temptation and be able to help us when we are tempted (Heb. 2:17–18; 4:15). He overcame the devil by using the same weapons available to us today: the Word of God ("It is written"), the power of the Spirit (v. 1; Luke 4:1), and prayer (Luke 3:21; 1 Cor. 10:13).

The Master (12–22). Having defeated "the strong man," Jesus now invaded his house and began to spoil his goods (12:24–30). He both obeyed the Word (vv. 15–16; Isa. 9:1–2) and preached it, calling men to become His disciples. Everyone must decide whether to follow Christ or make bargains with the devil (vv. 8–10). What is *your* decision?

The Healer (23–25). Our Lord's main ministry was teaching and preaching, but His compassion moved Him to minister to the physical needs of the people. How tragic that most of the people who followed Him wanted His services but not His sal-

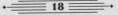

vation, the gifts but not the Giver; and these people are with us today.

> **❝**Let no man think himself to be holy because he is not tempted, for the holiest and highest in life have the most temptations. How much higher the hill is, so much is the wind there greater; so, how much higher the life is, so much the stronger is the temptation of the enemy.**❞**
>
> John Wycliffe

THE SERMON ON THE MOUNT

The Sermon on the Mount was our Lord's "ordination sermon" for His apostles (Luke 6:12ff.). The theme is God's righteousness as contrasted with the hypocritical righteousness of the scribes and Pharisees (5:17–20; Matt. 23). The sermon is not a second Law with new commandments. It goes much deeper than the Law because it deals with internal attitudes as well as outward actions. It presents a picture of the truly righteous person and shows the spiritual principles that control his or her life.

Jesus opened the sermon with a description of the truly righteous person (5:1–16). Then He defined what sin is (5:21–48) and what real righteousness is in the areas of worship (6:1–18) and wealth (6:19–34). He concluded with warnings against making hypocritical judgments (7:1–12), following false prophets (7:13–20), and failing to obey God's will (7:21–29).

You are not saved by trying to obey the Sermon on the Mount any more than you are saved by trying to keep the Ten Commandments. Because they involve inner attitudes, the demands of the Sermon on the Mount are much more difficult than those found in the law of Moses. Only the true believer in Jesus Christ can put the Sermon on the Mount into practice (Rom. 8:1–4).

MATTHEW 5

Citizens (1–12). We enter the kingdom through the new birth (John 3:1–16), but we enjoy the kingdom by living for those things that please God the most (6:33). The world (and worldly believers) would disagree with Christ's description of a blessed (happy) person, but the description is true just the same. God majors on character, and so should we.

Salt and light (13–16). Tasteless salt and hidden light are good for nothing! Salt arrests decay in our world, and light banishes darkness. Salt is hidden, but light is visible. Both are needed in the world, and both must give of themselves in order to serve.

Worshipers (17–26). If you bring anger to the altar, you cannot worship God, so get rid of the anger quickly. Angry feelings lead to angry words and deeds, and the result could be murder. (See Eph. 4:25–32.)

Surgeons (27–32). Obviously Jesus is not suggesting literal surgery, for the real problem is in the heart (v. 28). This is a vivid reminder that sin is terrible, and we are better off "maimed" than whole and going to hell. Deal drastically with sin!

Children of the Father (33–48). "What do you do more than others?" (v. 47). We must measure ourselves not by others but by the Father (v. 48). This includes our words (vv. 33–37), our responses to injuries (vv. 38–42), and our dealings with our enemies (vv. 43–48).

> **"**In taking revenge, a man is but even with his enemy;
> but in passing it over, he is superior.**"**
>
> Francis Bacon

MATTHEW 6

Praise (1–4). We should give only to please God and receive His praise. If we give to win the praise of others, or to be able to compliment ourselves (v. 3), we get the *immediate* reward—

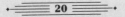

praise—but we lose the *eternal* reward. We cannot get our reward twice, so we must decide which one we want.

Prayer (5–15). Our public praying is only as good as our private praying, and our private praying should be secret (vv. 5–6), sincere (vv. 7–8), and systematic (vv. 9–13). The Lord's Prayer is a pattern for us to follow so that we will put God's concerns first and not forget to forgive others.

Possessions (16–34). We need *things* to live (v. 32), and God provides these things for us (v. 33); but acquiring things must not be the main goal of life. You are living for things when they capture your heart (vv. 19–21), divide your mind (vv. 22–23), and control your will (v. 24); and the result of this is *worry*. The solution is to put God first and start living with eternity's values in view.

Treasures in Heaven

We lay up treasures in heaven when we consider that all we have belongs to God and we use it to magnify His righteousness and advance His kingdom (Matt. 6:33). It means much more than merely giving offerings to God, although that is important. It means total stewardship of life so that God is in complete control and our one desire is to glorify Him. This is the secret of a unified life (Matt. 6:24) free of worry.

MATTHEW 7

Judges (1–12). One of the easiest ways to cover our sins is to judge others. It is not wrong to exercise discernment (v. 6), but we must start with ourselves. Often we are guilty of the sins we think we see in others (Rom. 2:1–3). We need prayer and love if we are to perform successful "eye surgery" on our brothers and sisters. We must treat them the way we want them to treat us.

Pilgrims (13–14). The gate into real life is narrow, and the way is difficult, so don't try to carry a lot of excess baggage. False teachers make the way easy and popular; if you truly follow Jesus, you pay a price and the way sometimes becomes lonely.

Trees (15–20). Life produces fruit, and good trees produce good fruit. There was a great deal of profession in the lives of the scribes and Pharisees, but no evidence of spiritual fruit.

Builders (21–29). To "build on the rock" means to obey the Word of God. *Saying* is not enough; there must be *doing* (James 1:22–25). If you claim to be a disciple of Jesus Christ, expect to have your profession tested in this life and the next. Fair-weather faith will not pass the test.

MATTHEW 8—9

In these two chapters, Matthew assembled several of our Lord's miracles and recorded them as proof that Jesus is the promised Messiah (1 Cor. 1:22; Isa. 35:4–6). In 8:17, he quoted Isaiah 53:4 and applied it to Christ's healing ministry while He was on earth. Some helpful lessons are evident in these miracles.

Growing in Your Faith

Some people have "no faith" (Mark 4:40), while others have "little faith" (Matt. 6:30). God wants us to have "great faith" (Matt. 8:10; 15:28). Faith is like a seed that grows if it is planted and cultivated in the heart (Matt. 17:20). The Word of God encourages faith (Rom. 10:17). As you exercise your faith in times of trial and testing, your faith grows and you glorify God (James 1:1–8; 1 Pet. 1:1–9). It is faith, not feeling, that gives the victory (1 John 5:1–5).

God is concerned with individuals. Jesus did not minister only to crowds (8:1; 9:36); He had time for individuals. He had compassion on people shunned by others. Peter and John had this same spirit: they ministered to thousands (Acts 2) and also took time for one beggar (Acts 3).

God can meet every need. Nothing is too hard for the Lord (Jer. 32:17). He can heal the sick and afflicted, calm the storm, cast out demons, and even raise the dead. Do you cast *every* care on Him (1 Pet. 5:7)?

Peter and Jesus

The healing of Peter's mother-in-law was the first of several miracles that Jesus performed especially for Peter. On two occasions, He enabled Peter to catch many fish (Luke 5:1–11; John 21:1–8), and He even helped him catch one fish with a coin in its mouth (Matt. 17:24–27). Jesus enabled Peter to walk on the water (Matt. 14:22–33). When Peter cut off the ear of Malchus, Jesus healed it (Luke 22:50–53); and He delivered Peter from prison and death (Acts 12). No wonder Peter wrote, "Casting all your care upon Him, for He cares for you" (1 Pet. 5:7).

God responds to faith. The centurion had *great* faith (8:10), while the disciples were guilty of *little* faith (8:26). The men who brought their friend exercised *cooperative* faith (9:2), while the sick woman had almost *superstitious* faith (9:21). Christ asks you the same question He asked the two blind men: "Do you believe that I am able to do this?" (9:28). What is your reply?

God's greatest concern is the salvation of sinners. The healing of the sick is a great miracle, and the raising of the dead an even greater one; but the salvation of the lost soul is

the greatest miracle of all, Jesus is the Great Physician who came to heal sinners (9:12–13), the Bridegroom who invites sinners to the wedding feast (9:14–17), and the Good Shepherd who has compassion on the struggling sheep (9:35–36).

God calls us to help Him reach the lost. Peter opened his home and Jesus healed many there (8:14–16), and Matthew used his home to introduce his friends to Jesus (9:9–17). The blind men who were healed spread the news about Jesus to the whole country (9:31). Jesus is seeking disciples (8:18–22) and harvesters (9:37–38) to help Him get the job done.

MATTHEW 10

If you start to pray for laborers (9:38), beware: you may become an answer to your own prayer! You pray, and then you are sent out!

Some of these instructions applied mainly to the apostles (vv. 5–15) and some to those serving just before the Lord's return (vv. 16–23). However, spiritual principles are here for all God's servants.

Christ calls and equips. If the Lord calls you, He will equip you for the task He wants you to fulfill. It has well been said, "The will of God does not send you where the grace of God cannot keep you."

Christ does not promise an easy life. It is a wonderful privilege to be an ambassador for the King, but there is a price to pay. We are sheep among wolves (v. 16), sword-bearers (vv. 34–36), and cross-bearers (vv. 37–39). The world hates us because it hates Him (vv. 24–25; Phil. 3:10).

Christ wants us to give freely to others (8). The apostles had power to do miracles, but even giving a cup of cold water is service to the Lord (v. 42). Everything we have is a gift from God (John 3:27; 1 Cor. 4:7) and must be shared lovingly with others. We must live by faith and trust Him to provide.

Christ can take away all fear. If you fear God, you need fear nothing else (vv. 27–31; Ps. 112). You are precious to your Father, and He will care for you. God's servants are immortal until their work is done.

Review the chapter and mark the promises you need to claim today.

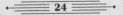

MATTHEW 11

John the Baptist was perplexed and perhaps discouraged. He had served God faithfully and yet was in prison. His work was ended, and he was not sure that Jesus was ministering in the right way. When you find yourself in a similar situation, do what John did: tell it to Jesus and wait for His word (vv. 4–6; Isa. 35:4–6). Isaiah 50:10 is a great promise to claim in dark days of disappointment.

John's disciples did not hear Jesus praise their leader. John was not a compromiser (a reed) or a celebrity; he was God's greatest prophet. John was in prison because of a cruel king and a crowd that was childish (vv. 16–19) instead of childlike (v. 25).

Leave the judgment to the Lord (vv. 20–24), and wait for Him to fulfill His perfect plan. You may think you have failed, but God will see to it that your work is blessed. In fact, John won people to Jesus long after he was dead and buried (John 10:40–42)! Surrender to Christ's loving yoke and you will experience His perfect rest (vv. 25–30).

MATTHEW 12

Hostility (1–8). The religious leaders were waiting for an opportunity to attack Jesus, and He deliberately gave it to them. What a tragedy to be burdened by legalism when you could enjoy the true Sabbath rest (11:28–30)! When Jesus is your Lord, all of life becomes a Sabbath and every place is God's temple, even a grain field.

Hypocrisy (9–14). The Pharisees were concerned about keeping the Sabbath but not about showing love to a man with a handicapping condition. Jesus wants mercy, not sacrifice (v. 7; Hos. 6:6; Mic. 6:6–8). Do you *use* people or *serve* them?

Victory (15–32). Jesus is the Stronger Man who has invaded Satan's house, overcome him, taken his weapons, and is now claiming his spoils (Eph. 1:15–23; Col. 2:15). Put on the armor and join Him in victory (Eph. 6:10ff.).

Neutrality (43–50). Beware an empty life! It is a standing invitation for Satan to go to work. In the spiritual war being waged today, you cannot be neutral. You are either for Him or against Him.

The Unpardonable Sin

The unpardonable sin is committed by people who resist the work of the Spirit and reject His witness concerning Jesus. It is a sin of the heart, not the lips, because what we say comes from the heart (Matt. 12:33–37). When the religious leaders allowed John the Baptist to be arrested and slain, they sinned against God the Father who sent him. When they crucified Christ, they sinned against God the Son. Jesus asked for their forgiveness (Luke 23:34), and God gave them another chance. When they persecuted the apostles and then killed Stephen, they sinned against the Holy Spirit who was working through them (Acts 7:51). That sin against the Spirit brought about the downfall of the nation. God can forgive all sins except the sin of rejecting His Son (John 3:36). God's children cannot commit an unpardonable sin, for all of their sins were forgiven when they trusted Jesus Christ (John 3:18; Rom. 8:1; Col. 2:13).

MATTHEW 13

These parables explain how God is at work in the world today. The kingdom of heaven is not the true church, for the kingdom of heaven contains both true and false, saved and

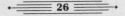

lost. The kingdom of heaven is made up of all who profess any kind of allegiance to the King.

God is sowing His Word in human hearts and looking for fruit (vv. 1–9, 18–23). He is sowing His people in the world where they can produce a harvest (vv. 24–30, 36–43). At the end of the age, He will separate the true from the false and the good from the bad.

Is your profession of Christ authentic? Or will you be seen as a counterfeit at the end of the age? (See Matt. 7:21–29.)

Does your heart receive the Word? The seed has life and power and can produce a harvest of blessing in your life. Do you hear it?

Can God "plant you" where He wants you? You are a seed containing His divine life, but a seed must be planted to produce fruit (John 12:23–28).

Do you share with others what He teaches you (51–52)? Truth must not be hoarded; it must be shared so that others can be saved and built up in the faith.

Receive the Truth	*The word parable comes from a Greek word that means "to throw alongside." Jesus used the familiar to teach the unfamiliar ("things new and old" Matt. 13:52). He did that not to hide the truth but to arouse interest in the truth (Matt. 13:13–15). He wanted to get the people to open their eyes and ears and receive the truth into their sluggish hearts.*

MATTHEW 14

Tell it to Jesus (1–12). The disciples of John the Baptist were stunned, so they shared their grief with Jesus. Life will bring its disappointments, and you must learn how to handle them. Jesus will help you (Ps. 55:22; 1 Peter 5:7).

Bring it to Jesus (13–21). The Twelve said, "Send them

away!" But Jesus said, "Bring what you have to Me!" Give Him your all, and He will use it to meet the need. He can do the impossible with whatever is wholly given to Him. You can even bring to Him *people* who need His touch (v. 35).

Look to Jesus (22–33). Some storms come because of our disobedience, but this one came because they obeyed Jesus. Peter *did* walk on the water; but when distracted by dangers around him, he took his eyes off Jesus. We look to Jesus by faith when we trust His word (Heb. 12:1–3). Beware distractions!

"He is nigh when He seems absent. He is watching when He seems blind. He is active when He seems idle.**"**

G. Campbell Morgan

MATTHEW 15

Our Lord's disciples never knew what would happen next! You can check your own responses to life's challenges as you consider how they handled three different situations.

Offended people (1–20). Jesus rejected the man-made traditions of the scribes and Pharisees because they focused on the outside and ignored the inner person. These men were plants that God did not plant (13:24–30) and blind guides who were leading people astray. "Let them alone!" was our Lord's counsel.

Persistent people (21–31). Again, the disciples were wrong. Jesus seemed to ignore the woman, but He wanted only to increase her faith. His delays are not His denials. Jesus was ministering in gentile territory, and the people "glorified the God of Israel" (v. 31).

Hungry people (32–39). The disciples had already forgotten the miracle of feeding the five thousand! When you are faced with a crisis, take time to review His past mercies; remind yourself that He does not change.

Try to respond to people today the way Jesus responded. Ask Him for discernment.

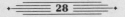

MATTHEW 16

Are you guilty of these misunderstandings?

About the times (1–4). People believe the weather report but not God's Word! They fail to see what God is doing in His world. Keep your eyes open, and ask God for wisdom to understand His plan.

About false doctrine (5–12). Jesus compared false doctrine to *yeast*. It appears small and insignificant, but it grows secretly and soon permeates everything (Gal. 5:9). The only remedy is to remove it (1 Cor. 5:6–7).

About Jesus Christ (13–20). The crowd is confused about Jesus; do not follow it. Instead, let the Father reveal the Savior to you (11:25–27), and confess Him before others. He is the Son of God.

Peter

The name Peter means "a stone" (John 1:40–42). All of God's people are "living stones," but Jesus is the Rock (1 Pet. 2:4–8; Acts 4:11–12; Ps. 118:22), and His church is built on Him (1 Cor. 3:11). Whoever confesses faith in Christ becomes a living stone built into the spiritual temple (Eph. 2:19–22). Peter was given not the keys of heaven, for Jesus holds them (Rev. 1:18), but the "keys of the kingdom of heaven" (Matt. 16:19). He had the privilege of opening "the door of faith" (Acts 14:27) to the Jews at Pentecost (Acts 2), the Samaritans (Acts 8:14ff.), and the Gentiles (Acts 10).

About discipleship (21–28). In his misguided attempt to keep Jesus from suffering and dying, Peter the stone became Peter the stumbling block. Confessing Christ must lead to fol-

lowing Christ. The world encourages you to pamper yourself, but the Lord calls you to deny yourself. The only way to live is to die to self and follow Christ by faith.

MATTHEW 17

Listen to the King (1-13)! This event was a picture of the coming kingdom (16:27-28) and a proof that Jesus Christ is indeed the Son of the living God. The Law (Moses) and the prophets (Elijah) all converge in Him (Heb. 1:1-2). But the thing Peter remembered most was the emphasis on the unchanging Word of God (2 Pet. 1:16-21). The memory of visions will fade, but the Word endures forever. Hear Him!

Trust the King (14-21)! Jesus gave the disciples power to cast out demons (10:1, 8), but their unbelief and lack of prayer (vv. 20-21) robbed them of the power they needed. We cannot stay on the mountain of glory; there are needs to be met in the valley.

Obey the King (22-27)! The tax was an annual assessment of the Jewish men for the support of the temple (Exod. 30:11-16). Jesus affirmed His kingship by controlling a coin and a fish, but He affirmed His servanthood by submitting to their demands. "Lest we offend them" (v. 27) is a good principle when you lay aside your rights, but be careful not to set aside God's truth (15:12-14).

MATTHEW 18

Greatness (1-14). A child totally depends on others and must live by faith. An unspoiled child accepts his position in life, enjoys it, and does not try to act like someone older (Ps. 131). "He will be greatest who has the least idea he is great," wrote A. H. McNeile.

The way we treat children (including those who are "children in the faith") indicates how much humility we practice. Do we receive them (v. 5) or despise them (v. 10)? Do we imitate them (vv. 3-4) or cause them to stumble by our bad example (vv. 6-9)? It was a *sheep*, not a *lamb*, that went astray (vv. 10-14)!

Truthfulness (15-20). "Speaking the truth in love" (Eph. 4:15) is the secret of maintaining Christian fellowship. The

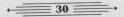

longer we resist, the more people we involve in the problem (Matt. 5:21-26). Humility and honesty must work together in producing harmony.

Forgiveness (21-35). Peter wanted a rule to obey, which shows he was not in the spirit of what Jesus taught (Rom. 12:8-10). The parable is not about salvation but about forgiveness among God's people. We are to forgive others because God has forgiven us (Eph. 4:32; Col. 3:13), *and He has forgiven us at great cost to Himself!* It is possible to *receive* forgiveness but not truly *experience* forgiveness in our hearts; therefore, we have a hard time *sharing* forgiveness with others.

When you have an unforgiving spirit, you put yourself in prison spiritually and emotionally; you pay dearly for the luxury of carrying a grudge. Is it worth it?

❝He who cannot forgive breaks the bridge over which he himself must pass.**❞**

George Herbert

MATTHEW 19

Let Jesus heal your marriage (1-12). Some practices are lawful but not biblical, so follow the principles given in Scripture. God's original plan was one man for one woman for all of life (Gen. 2:18-25), but He made a concession for Israel and permitted divorce (Deut. 24:1-4). Divorce is not given as the solution to the problem. It takes a change of heart for two people to make a new beginning, and only Jesus can change hearts. Before you run away, run to God and seek His help.

Let Jesus bless your family (13-15). Children want to come to Jesus (v. 14), but too often adults get in the way. The best parents make it easy for their children to come to Christ, love Him, and receive His blessing.

Let Jesus have your all (16-30). The wealthy young man had much in his favor, but he thought too highly of himself and was not really honest before God. Money stood between him

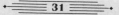

and salvation, and he would not repent and renounce his false god. You never lose when you give everything to Jesus. He blesses you in this life and in the life to come.

❝A good marriage is not a contract between two persons but a sacred covenant between three. Too often Christ is never invited to the wedding and finds no room in the home.❞

Donald T. Kauffman

MATTHEW 20

What shall we have (19:27—20:16)? The parable is not about salvation, for we cannot work for salvation; nor is it about rewards, for we do not all receive the same reward. The story concerns the selfish attitude implicit in Peter's question. The key to the parable is that the first workers hired *demanded a contract and insisted on knowing how much they would get.* The other workers trusted the landowner. If you ask God for a contract, you will only rob yourself, for He is generous with His workers. Be faithful to do your job and avoid watching the other workers, and He will deal with you generously.

What do you wish (20:17-28)? Salome remembered His promise (19:28) and claimed it for her two sons. But she forgot what Jesus had just said about the cross (20:17-19). She should have known that the only way to glory is through suffering (1 Pet. 5:10). You do not *pray* for a throne; you *pay* for it. Beware selfish prayers: the Lord may answer them. James was the first apostle to be martyred (Acts 12:1-2), and John experienced great trial as a Roman prisoner (Rev. 1:9).

What do you want Me to do for you (20:29-34)? They knew what they wanted, and they trusted Him for it. Do you know what you want when you come to Him in prayer? Do you persist even if others try to discourage you? What a promise we have in Hebrews 4:16!

The Last Week

Traditionally, the events during our Lord's last week are as follows: Sunday—He entered Jerusalem as King. Monday—He cleansed the temple and cursed the fig tree. Tuesday—He debated with the Jewish leaders and gave the Olivet Discourse (Matt. 24—25). Wednesday—He rested. Thursday—He had the Last Supper; He was arrested in the Garden. Friday—He was crucified and buried. Saturday—He lay in the tomb. Sunday—He arose from the dead. Keep in mind that the Jewish day begins with sundown, so that their Friday begins Thursday evening.

MATTHEW 21:1—22:14

The King (21:1-11). The people were blind to their Scriptures (Zech. 9:9). They praised Him with Psalm 118:26 but overlooked verses 22-23, which Jesus quoted later (v. 42). Beware knowing the Bible but not knowing the Lord when He is at work in your midst.

The Judge (21:12-22). Jesus cleansed the temple and cursed the fig tree, two "unusual acts" for Him who came not to judge but to save (Isa. 28:21). Like the temple, Israel was corrupt within; and like the fig tree, it was fruitless without. A church can become a "den of thieves" if that is where we go to cover up our sins (Isa. 56:7; 1:10-20; Jer. 7:11). A person whose life is "nothing but leaves" is in danger of judgment, for Christ seeks fruit (Matt. 7:15-20).

The Son (21:23-41). Jesus has authority because He is the Son of God! The vineyard is Israel (Isa. 5) whose leaders did not respect the Son when He came. The nation rejected the Father when they refused the witness of John, and now they were about to reject the Son.

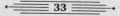

The Stone (21:42–46). The Jewish leaders pronounced their own sentence. Jesus quoted Psalm 118:22–23 to prove that their sins would not hinder His victory (Isa. 8:14–15; Dan. 2:34; Acts 4:11; 1 Pet. 2:9). If only they had become like the children and praised the Lord instead of fighting Him (Matt. 21:15–16; Ps. 8:2)!

The Bridegroom (22:1–14). The rejected Son is resurrected and reigns in glory. He is the Bridegroom who wants everybody to come to His feast. Israel's rejection of the invitation led to the destruction of Jerusalem (v. 7). But the invitation is still open today. Just be sure not to wear your self-righteousness (Isa. 64:6); let Him provide the garment of His righteousness (Isa. 61:10; 2 Cor. 5:21).

MATTHEW 22:15–46

His enemies questioned Jesus, hoping to get Him in trouble with Rome. After Passover, they could have Him arrested and tried. But how can mortal man question God and hope to win (Job 38:1–3)? What arrogance—and what ignorance!

Jesus asked the key question: "Who is your Lord?" (vv. 41–46; Ps. 110). If Jesus Christ is your Lord, the other questions pose no problem. You will be a good citizen (vv. 15–22; Rom. 13); you will not worry about the hereafter (vv. 23–33); and you will love God and your neighbor (vv. 34–40).

People who like to argue usually lack humility and need to submit to Christ (Phil. 2:1–11). Although it is good to ponder the great questions of life, it is also good to admit our ignorance and to worship Christ "in whom are hidden all the treasures of wisdom and knowledge" (Col. 2:3).

MATTHEW 23

The Word of God has authority even if the people who teach it lack integrity (vv. 1–3). Our Lord's standard is that we both *do* and *teach* His truth (5:17–20; 1 Thess. 2:10–12). Those who practice hypocrisy erode their character and do untold damage to others. The tragedy is that hypocrisy blinds people (vv. 16–19, 24, 26) so that they cannot see the Lord, themselves, or other people.

The God of the Pharisees is not the God of the Bible. He is a rigorous Law Giver who pays back those who pay Him. He is not "the God of all grace" (1 Pet. 5:10) or the loving Father who cares for His children (Ps. 103:1–14).

The Pharisees were blind to themselves. *They* were right, and everybody else was wrong. Because they majored on the externals, they never saw the rottenness in their hearts (vv. 25–28). Because they majored on the minor details, they ignored the great principles of the Word (v. 23).

Hypocrites never see the damage done to others: closing doors of blessing (v. 13); defiling those who touch them (v. 27); giving people a wrong sense of values (vv. 16–22). No wonder Jesus wept! These "woes" were born of anguish, not anger; and perhaps He is weeping over you and me.

Hypocrisy

Failing to reach your goals or to be all that you want to be is not hypocrisy. Pretending that you have "arrived" is hypocrisy. The word hypocrite *comes from the Greek word for the mask worn by an actor. Hypocrites deliberately play a part so people will think they are more spiritual than they really are. The remedy for hypocrisy is honesty with yourself and with God (1 John 1:5–10).*

THE OLIVET DISCOURSE

Our Lord's words about the desolation of the temple (23:37–39) prompted the disciples to ask Him about the future of the city, the temple, and the nation. In 24:1–35, the theme is the Tribulation ("day of the Lord") that will come upon the world in the last days. Jesus explained the events of the first half of the tribulation (24:1–14) and the last half (24:15–28); and then He announced His return to earth after the Tribulation (24:29–35).

In 24:1–35, the emphasis is on *the signs of His coming to the earth* and is directed primarily to Israel (vv. 15–28), telling the people to watch and be ready. But these words have a message for the church today, because "coming events cast their shadows before." We are looking for the Savior and not for signs (Phil. 3:20), because He can come at any time; but as we see these things developing in our world, we are encouraged to expect Him soon.

Matthew 24:36—25:46 focuses on the church rather than Israel. The emphasis is not on signs but on the fact that Jesus can return at any time (24:36, 44, 50). When He comes, He will reckon with His servants and reward those who have been faithful; it behooves us to be ready.

MATTHEW 24

When you listen to the news and see the tensions and troubles in today's world, keep in mind the warnings that the Lord gave.

Do not be deceived (4, 11). People will make grandiose claims and promises and will deceive many. You have the Word of God to enlighten you (Isa. 8:20) and the Holy Spirit to teach you (John 16:13–15), so you should not go astray (1 John 2:18–29).

Do not be discouraged (6). Political and natural disturbances have always been a part of world history, so do not allow them to discourage you. They are "the beginning of sorrows" (v. 8). The word translated "sorrows" means "birthpangs." The world's troubles are pregnant with possibilities! God is still on the throne!

Do not be defeated (13). This has to do with faithfulness under testing until the Lord returns. Do not let the lawlessness around you rob you of your fervor (v. 12). A lost world around you needs to hear the gospel (v. 14), so get busy!

Do not be doubtful (34–35). Religious leaders will come and go, stand and fall; but the Word will not change. Believe it, obey it, and hold to it—no matter what others may say or do. Your Bible is God's light in this dark world (2 Pet. 1:19–21).

Do not be distracted (42). We "watch" when we stay alert and remind ourselves that our Lord may come at any time. When in your heart you delay His coming (v. 48), you start to lose your effectiveness and witness. Keep watching and working!

MATTHEW 25

When Jesus Christ returns, it will be a time of *separation:* the wise will be separated from the foolish, the faithful servants from the unfaithful, the blessed (sheep) from the cursed (goats). The wise virgins had oil and were prepared to meet the Bridegroom. Many people profess to be Christians but do not have the Holy Spirit (Rom. 8:9) and are not born again. They may mingle with the saved, but they are not really one of them; and they will not enter into the marriage feast.

His coming also means *evaluation.* As we wait for the Lord to return, we must invest our lives and earn dividends for His glory. Christ gives us opportunities that match our abilities, and the one-talent servant is just as important as the five-talent servant. The key is *faithfulness* (1 Cor. 4:2), for God measures us against ourselves and not against the other servants. Are you afraid to step out by faith and take some risks for God?

When Christ returns, it will be a time of *commendation.* We will be surprised to learn about ministries we performed that we thought were insignificant but that He will reward. This parable is not teaching salvation by good works. Christ's sheep know that they are sheep (John 10:14, 27–30), but they do not always realize what their service means to Christ. We will experience some surprises in that day!

“*Great services reveal our possibilities; small services our consecration.***”**

George Morrison

MATTHEW 26

Life presents us with many opportunities; how we respond to them depends on what we love and what we look for in life.

The Jewish leaders looked for opportunity to destroy Jesus, while at the same time Jesus was anticipating the opportunity to obey His Father and bring Him glory.

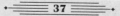

Mary used the opportunity she had for expressing her devotion to Christ, but Judas used that same opportunity to criticize her. Nothing given in love to Jesus is ever wasted. Judas was the one who ended up wasting his life!

Jesus eagerly anticipated the opportunity to be with His disciples, even though He knew one would betray Him, one would deny Him, and all would forsake Him. He sought to help them and prepare them for the trial before them.

Peter missed his opportunities to become strong and be a victor. He boasted when he should have listened (vv. 32–35), slept when he should have prayed (vv. 36–46), fought when he should have surrendered (vv. 47–56), and followed when he should have fled for safety (vv. 57–75; note v. 31). But when the opportunity came for him to repent, he wept.

No matter what others did, Jesus was in complete command and knew how to make the most of every opportunity. "Not as I will, but as You will" is the secret (v. 39). God will give you many opportunities today. Use them wisely!

> **❝**God's best gifts are not things but opportunities. What we call adversity, God calls opportunity.**❞**

MATTHEW 27

Jesus is the example to follow when you suffer unjustly (1 Pet. 2:18–23).

He did not reply when accused (11–14). In this, He fulfilled Isaiah 53:7. There is a time to speak and a time to be silent (Eccles. 3:7), and we must exercise discernment. One thing is sure: no matter what He said, they would not have believed Him.

He did not retaliate when abused (15–31). He had the power to destroy those who mocked Him; in fact, legions of angels would have delivered Him. But it was the Father's will that He suffer as He did, and Jesus was obedient to His Father's will.

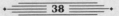

He did not accept the cup (32–38). The narcotic drink would have helped deaden the pain, but Jesus refused it. He drank the cup of suffering instead.

He did not come down from the cross (40–44). Had He come down from the cross, the people still would not have believed in Him. And if He saved Himself, He could not save others (John 12:23–28). First the suffering, then the glory; first the cross, then the crown. Remember that the next time you are tempted to take the easy way.

"*Leave out the cross, and you have killed the religion of Jesus. Atonement by the blood of Jesus is not an arm of Christian truth; it is the heart of it.***"**

Charles Haddon Spurgeon

MATTHEW 28

The message of the empty tomb is, "Do not be afraid!"

He overcomes His enemies (1–5). In His death and resurrection, our Lord defeated the world (John 16:33), the flesh (Rom. 6:1–7), the devil (John 12:31), and death itself (1 Cor. 15:50–58). You need not be afraid of life or death, time or eternity (Rev. 1:17–18).

He keeps His promises (6–7). Because His followers forgot His resurrection promise, they were sorrowing instead of rejoicing. The Lord always keeps His promises, no matter how dark the day may be.

He goes before you (7–10). When the women ran to share the message, they met the Lord; you always meet Him in the path of obedience. The Shepherd goes before the sheep and prepares the way for them (John 10:4). You have a living and victorious Savior who has everything under control. Trust Him!

He is our Lord (11–20). He has *all authority*; He commands us to take the gospel to *all nations*; and He promises to be with us *always*. What more assurance could we want? We are His ambassadors (2 Cor. 5:20) and should be faithful to Him in *all things*.

The Resurrection

The resurrection of Jesus Christ is a vital part of the gospel message, for a dead Christ can save nobody (1 Cor. 15:1–19). The empty tomb is proof that He is the Son of God (Rom. 1:4); that believers have a future inheritance (1 Pet. 1:3ff.); that we will once again meet Christians who have died (1 Thess. 4:14–18); that our Christian ministry is not in vain (1 Cor. 15:50–58); and that Jesus Christ will one day judge lost sinners (Acts 17:30–31). The early church bore witness of the resurrection of Jesus Christ (Acts 1:22; 4:2, 33), and so should we today.

MARK

◆

John Mark was the cousin of Barnabas (Col. 4:10; Acts 4:36–37; 11:19–30) and the son of Mary, a leading woman in the Jerusalem church (Acts 12:12). He helped Paul and Barnabas on their first missionary journey (Acts 12:25—13:5) but for some reason did not remain with them (Acts 13:13). That failure caused Paul and Barnabas to separate, but Barnabas gave Mark another chance (Acts 15:36–41). In later years, Mark became one of Paul's associates (Philem. 24); and Paul commended him for his work (2 Tim. 4:11). It all ended well.

First Peter 5:13 suggests that John Mark was converted through Peter's ministry. Many Bible scholars believe that Mark's gospel is a record of Peter's reports of the ministry of Christ, presenting Jesus Christ as the Servant of God (Mark 10:45). Mark often used the word *immediately*, for he describes the work of a Servant who was busy obeying His Father and meeting the needs of people (1:10, 12, 20–21, etc.). Mark wrote with the Romans in mind, an active people who admired accomplishment.

After a brief introduction (1:1–13), the book tells of Christ's ministry in Galilee (1:14—9:50), His journey to Jerusalem (chap. 10), His ministry in Jerusalem, climaxing with His crucifixion (chaps. 11–15), and His resurrection and ascension (chap. 16).

MARK 1

Even a servant must have credentials, and our Lord has the very best. His coming was prophesied by Isaiah (40:3) and Malachi (3:1) and announced by John the Baptist. The Father and the Holy Spirit commended Him (vv. 9–11), and Satan could not defeat Him (vv. 12–13). He is a Servant you can trust.

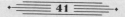

But what can He do? What is His work? He can guide your life and make it a success (vv. 16–20). He can overcome Satan (vv. 21–28) and sickness (vv. 29–34, 40–45) and use you to bring the message of salvation to a lost and needy world (vv. 35–39). You can be a servant of the Servant and share in His wonderful work.

Where did the Servant get His power? He depended on the Holy Spirit (v. 12) and prayer (v. 35). He did not allow the demands of the work to rob Him of the time He needed to renew His strength. If the holy Son of God needed to pray, how much more do you need to pray! In the Lord's service, you cannot "run on empty." (See Isa. 40:28–31.)

MARK 2

Consider the unique ministries of God's Servant, Jesus Christ.

He forgives our sins (1–12). Imagine a servant having such authority! The healing of the body is a great miracle, but it does not last. The forgiveness of sin is God's greatest miracle, for it lasts forever and accomplishes the greatest good. The Servant forgives us *and pays the price for the miracle!*

Garments of New Life

Our first parents tried to cover their sins with garments they made (Gen. 3:7), but God would not accept them. Instead, He clothed them with skins (Gen. 3:21); blood had to be shed (Heb. 9:22). Jesus did not come to do a patchwork job on our lives; He came to make us whole. We have been raised from the dead (Eph. 2:1–10); and like Lazarus, we must take off the old garments of death and put on the garments of new life (John 11:44; Col. 3:1ff.).

He fellowships with "sinners" (13–22). Why? Because they are sick, and He is the only Physician who can heal them. They are hungry and lonely, and He is the Bridegroom who asks them to His wedding feast. Their lives are in tatters, and He wants to give them a new robe of righteousness. Others may be able to patch up life, but He alone can give new life.

He frees us from bondage (23–28). He is Lord of the Sabbath, the Giver of rest (Matt. 11:28–30). Man's religious traditions can be a terrible yoke of bondage; but when you follow the Lord, you experience freedom and rest.

MARK 3

Some resist the Servant (1–6, 20–30). The religious leaders were more concerned about protecting their tradition than helping a man with a handicapping condition. In spite of all that Jesus did and said, they hardened their hearts and resisted His ministry, even to the extent of accusing Him of being in league with Satan. In the end, *they* cooperated with the evil one!

Some assist the Servant (7–19). The crowds were so large that Jesus had to empower His disciples to help Him in ministry. There is a job for everyone, even if only giving Him a little boat to use (v. 9). If you want to assist Him, remember that the most important thing is *being with Him* (v. 14). As He said,"Without Me, you can do nothing" (John 15:5).

Some mistrust the Servant (vv. 31–35). Mary bore other children after the birth of Jesus, but they did not believe in Him (John 7:1–5). Even His mother seemed to have doubts about her "popular" Son who was arousing the anger of the leaders (v. 35). But Jesus was doing the will of God, and so should we (v. 35).

MARK 4

Receiving God's Word (1–25). Even when we read the Bible, we should *hear* the voice of God speaking to our hearts. It must be personal. Never treat the Bible like any other book (1 Thess. 2:13). Jesus warns us to take heed *that* we hear (v. 9), *what* we hear (v. 24), and *how* we hear (Luke 8:18). The more of the Word we receive and share, the more God will give to us.

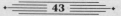

Reaping God's harvest (26–34). It is our job to sow the seed; we cannot make the seed germinate and produce a harvest. Even a busy farmer must sleep and let God work! However, when the harvest is ready, we must be alert and reap it, or the harvest may be lost (John 4:35–38).

Relying on God's power (35–41). Our faith in His Word is tested in the storms of life. If the disciples had really trusted His Word (v. 35), they would not have panicked and accused Him of not caring. You can trust His Word, for it will never fail.

MARK 5

The Servant comes to us (1–20). Jesus went through a storm to get to two demoniacs (Matt. 8:28) who needed his help. The demons begged not to be sent to the pit (v. 10), the citizens begged Jesus to leave (v. 17), and one healed man begged to be allowed to go with Jesus (v. 18). The citizens were concerned more with financial profit than with spiritual benefit. Imagine asking Jesus to leave you!

We can come to the Servant (21–34). All kinds of people came to the feet of Jesus. A well-known synagogue leader and an anonymous sick woman could find help there. Perhaps the woman's faith was a bit superstitious, but the Lord still honored it. If you cannot grasp His hand, touch the hem of His garment. The first step of faith, no matter how weak, will lead to greater blessings.

The Servant will go with us (35–43). No situation is so desperate that Jesus cannot work. Disease, delays, and even death are under His control. Jesus goes with you to the place of disappointment and sorrow and meets your needs. No matter how depressing your situation may appear, "Do not be afraid; only believe" (v. 36). The Servant is working for you.

MARK 6

The Servant cannot work (1–29). His neighbors were amazed at what Jesus said and did, but Jesus was amazed at their unbelief that would not let Him do more: "According to your faith let it be to you" (Matt. 9:29; Ps. 78:41). Ask God to strengthen your faith so that you can glorify Him (Rom. 4:20–

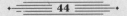

21). Our Lord's response to their unbelief was to send out His disciples to minister. Herod silenced one voice, but he could not silence the Word of God (Col. 4:2-4).

The Servant cannot rest (30-44). God's servants become weary as they work (John 4:6) and must care for the body. But when you have a compassionate heart, you will not have an idle hand. Our Lord interrupted His vacation to meet the needs of the people. He need not interrupt anything today, because caring for us is His constant ministry (Heb. 7:25).

The Servant cannot pray (45-56). After such a demanding time of ministry, Jesus had to go apart to pray (v. 46; 1:35). But once again, He was interrupted, this time by the plight of His disciples in the midst of the sea (v. 48). And it was the disciples who were amazed (v. 51)! Jesus intercedes for you and knows your situation. He will come to you, care for you, and lead you into His peace.

MARK 7

Defilement (1-23). Unless we are very careful, religious rituals can create serious problems. They may be given as much authority as God's Word (v. 7) and even replace God's Word (v. 9). They may give a false confidence that what you do on the outside will somehow change the inside. But the heart must be changed, and external rituals cannot do that. The heart can be purified only by faith (Acts 15:9).

Distance (24-30). Jesus healed both the centurion's servant (Matt. 8:1-13) and this woman's demonized daughter *from a distance*. Both were Gentiles, and the Gentiles were "at a distance" spiritually; but Jesus would erase that distance at the cross (Eph. 2:11-22). As you pray for those far from you, or far from the Lord, remember that He can send His Word and do mighty works (Ps. 107:20).

Deliverance (31-37). The miracles of healing this deaf man and healing a blind man (8:22-26) are recorded only by Mark. Both were in gentile territory, which would interest his Roman readers; both were performed away from the crowd; and both were performed despite difficulty. The Servant can work at a distance or when we bring people to Him, and He does not fail.

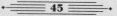

MARK 8

Defective faith (vv. 1–10). The disciples didn't know what to do with the hungry crowd, yet they had seen Jesus feed the five thousand (6:30–44). They apparently "soon forgot His works; they did not wait for His counsel" (Ps. 106:13). Each work that He does should encourage you to trust Him to help you solve the next problem. Keep a long memory for His mercies and a short one for your failures.

Defective understanding (11–21). The disciples did not perceive what He meant by the leaven (vv. 13–21). The blindness of the Pharisees does not surprise us (vv. 11–12), but why were His followers so blind? Like Israel of old, the disciples saw His acts but did not understand His ways (Ps. 103:7). Ask God to give you spiritual insight.

Defective sight (22–26). This is the only healing miracle recorded that took place in stages. Bethsaida was under judgment (Matt. 11:21–24), so Jesus took the man out of there and told him not to go back. Be careful where you send people whose eyes have been opened to Jesus and His mercy.

Defective devotion (27–38). One minute, Peter is inspired from heaven (Matt. 16:17); and the next minute, his tongue is ignited from hell (v. 33; James 3:6). Peter saw only shame in the Cross, but Jesus saw glory. Peter saw defeat, but Jesus saw great victory. Never be afraid or ashamed to be His disciple and bear your cross, for Jesus bore it first.

MARK 9

Consider some paradoxes of the Christian life.

Glory out of suffering (1–13). What happened on the Mount of Transfiguration was a confirmation of the testimony Peter gave. But it was also a revelation of the glory of the Cross (Gal. 6:14). First the suffering, then the glory. When you read 1 Peter, you discover that Peter learned his lesson well (1:6–8, 11; 4:12–16; 5:1, 10). Satan offers you glory without suffering (Matt. 4:8–10), but it ends up suffering without glory.

Victory out of defeat (14–29). Their failure to deliver the boy grieved the Lord, gave support to the enemy, and robbed God of glory. The nine disciples who were left behind had neglected their spiritual disciplines and lost their power (v. 29; 6:7). When you find yourself defeated, turn to Him for victory and discover where you went wrong.

Greatness out of service (30–41). This is a key passage in Mark's gospel because it emphasizes the importance of service. Do not aim for human greatness; aim to be more like Jesus Christ. Do not measure yourself by other servants (vv. 38–41); measure yourself by Him.

Gain out of loss (42–50). If you pamper sin in your life, you will lose your "salty" character and not be able to affect others for Christ. Deal drastically with sin as a surgeon does with a cancerous tumor. You gain by losing.

❝*One reason sin flourishes is that it is treated like a cream puff instead of a rattlesnake!***❞**

Billy Sunday

MARK 10

How far can I go (1–16)? The rabbis didn't agree on their interpretation of the divorce law (Deut. 24:1–4), one school being lenient and the other strict. When you live "by permission," you are tempted to follow those who tell you what you want to hear. Our Lord led the Pharisees back to God's original plan and interpreted it for them.

How much can I keep (17–27)? The rich young man was looking for a bargain, the best of both worlds; but he was doomed to failure. Calculation and crucifixion do not agree. At Calvary, there was no bargaining—just Jesus giving His all.

How much will we get (28–45)? Jesus promises to reward all who faithfully follow Him, but He warns against having rewards as your only motive for service. If you are His disciple, expect a cross, a cup, and a baptism, for the servant is not greater than his Lord. The important question is, "How much can we give?"

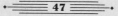

> **❝***Has He taken over in your heart? Perhaps He resides there, but does He preside there?***❞**

Vance Havner

MARK 11

Honor (1–11). The donkey was a royal animal, and the event was a coronation celebration (1 Kings 1:32–40). It was the only time our Lord permitted a public demonstration in His honor, and He did it to fulfill prophecy (Zech. 9:9) and turn the people's hearts back to the Word of God. They did not listen. What changes would Jesus make if He entered our places of worship today?

Hunger (12–14, 20–26). The fig tree pictures Israel, taking up space but not producing fruit (Luke 13:6–9). When we stop bearing fruit, the problem always starts with the roots (v. 20; Matt. 3:10). Jesus reminds us that we must have faith and forgiveness when we pray, or God will not answer.

Holiness (15–19). The psalmist proclaimed, "Holiness adorns Your house" (Ps. 93:5). But unholiness made the temple a place for thieves to hide! The leaders were not *praying;* they were *preying* and using religion only to make money.

Honesty (27–33). The leaders had not been honest with John the Baptist, and now they refused to be honest with Jesus. When we obey, God teaches us more (John 7:17); if we disobey, we close the door on God's truth.

MARK 12

Each family chose its Passover lamb on the tenth day of the month and carefully examined it until the fourteenth day to be sure it had no defects (Exod. 12:1–6). During His last week of public ministry, God's Lamb (John 1:29) was examined in various ways, and He passed every test. No guile was found in His mouth (Isa. 53:9).

In His replies, Jesus revealed to them who He was; yet they

would not accept the truth. He is the Son sent by the Father (vv. 1–9) and the Stone rejected by the builders (vv. 10–11; Ps. 118:22–23; Acts 4:11). His enemies were so intent on destroying Jesus that they did not realize they were destroying only themselves.

All political questions (vv. 13–17) and hypothetical doctrinal questions (vv. 18–27) are chaff compared to the most important question of all: Is Jesus Christ your Lord (vv. 35–37) and do you love Him (vv. 28–34)?

If you were to point out the spiritual people in this chapter, would you indicate the pious scribes (vv. 38–40) or the poor widow (vv. 41–44)? Read Revelation 2:9 and 3:17.

On Giving　　　*The Lord watches how we give (Mark 12:41–44) and examines the motives of the heart (Matt. 6:1–4). He also sees how much we give and measures the proportion, not the portion (1 Cor. 16:2). An old epitaph reads, "What I gave, I have. What I spent, I had. What I kept, I lost."*

MARK 13

This is Mark's version of the Olivet Discourse (Matt. 24—25), written with gentile readers in mind (v. 14). If we are to be ready and faithful in these last days, we must heed the admonitions of Jesus.

Take heed that no one deceives you (5). Political and geological disruption will give false prophets and false Christs great opportunity to deceive people. Persecution against God's people will either strengthen us or weaken us.

Take heed to what Jesus taught (23). The Word of God is the only dependable light in this dark world (2 Pet. 1:19). Jesus has told us beforehand what to expect and what to avoid, and we must heed His words. His Word is dependable and durable, so trust it.

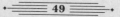

Take heed, watch, and pray (33). During the tribulation period, various signs will signal Christ's return to earth; but believers today are looking for the Savior and not for signs. "Be alert and keep praying!" is His admonition. "Do the work I have given you to do." You want to be found faithful when He comes, and He could come today.

MARK 14

Preparation for betrayal (1–2, 10–11). Judas solved the chief priests' problem by offering to lead them to Jesus. But how do you "conveniently" betray the Son of God? Is it not a *costly* endeavor in every way?

Preparation for burial (1–9). Mary's act of worship brought joy to the heart of Jesus and malice to the heart of Judas, who wanted the money she had spent (John 12:6). Other women came to anoint Him *after* His burial (16:1), but Mary did it when He could be encouraged by her love.

Preparation for fellowship (12–26). It meant much to Jesus to spend those hours with His disciples. He loved them (John 13:1), and their presence encouraged Him. He took the cup and the bread of the Passover and transformed them into memorials of His own blood and body, for He wanted the disciples to remember Him.

Preparation for danger (27–31, 66–72). The good fellowship in the Upper Room made the Twelve forget the danger outside, so Jesus gave them warning. Peter was not the only one who boasted and felt self-confident: "And they all said likewise" (v. 31). Heed His warnings; He knows what is coming.

Preparation for death (32–65). Jesus' prayers reveal the conflict in His holy soul as He faced bearing the sins of the world on the cross. When you have a Gethsemane experience, pray what He prayed: "Not what I will, but what You will" (v. 36). Peter had a sword, but Jesus took a cup. You need not fear the cup the Father has prepared for you. Jesus could submit to the abuse of men because He had already submitted to the will of God.

MARK 15

When you face the unjust assaults of an evil world, remember Jesus. The world says, "Defend yourself!" but Jesus was

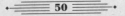

silent (vv. 1–5). The world says, "Pamper yourself!" but Jesus refused the drug (v. 23). The world says, "Save yourself!" but Jesus remained on the cross and finished the work the Father gave Him to do (v. 30).

Simon and the Cross

Simon of Cyrene had probably come to Jerusalem to celebrate Passover (Acts 2:10), and he met the Lamb of God! It seems certain that he was converted and went home to lead his two sons to faith in Christ. These men were known to Mark's Roman readers, so they must have become leaders in the church (Rom. 16:13). The next time your plans are interrupted and you have to carry another cross, remember what Simon did for Jesus—and what Jesus did for Simon.

Jesus Gave Himself

The devil told Jesus, "Serve Yourself!" (Matt. 4:3–4). Peter said, "Pity Yourself!" (Matt. 16:21–23). His unsaved relatives said, "Show Yourself!" (John 7:4). The crowd at Calvary said, "Save Yourself!" But Jesus was deaf to all those appeals and gave Himself.

The chief priests were guilty of *envy* (v. 10), and Pilate was guilty of *compromise* (v. 15). Their sins led to the release of an evil man (v. 15), the embarrassment of an innocent man (v. 21), and the death of a good Man (v. 25); yet envy and compromise are not looked upon as terrible sins today. Should they be?

Man was doing his worst, but God was doing His best and fulfilling His Word (vv. 28, 34): "But where sin abounded, grace abounded much more" (Rom. 5:20). And He did it for you and me!

MARK 16

He arose (1–8). Because they forgot His resurrection promises, the women were in sorrow and worrying about the future: "Who will roll away the stone?" When they learned that Jesus was alive, their first response was fear and not faith; but then they became the first heralds of the Resurrection. The angel had a special word for Peter (v. 7) who was no doubt still grieving his sins. The living Christ gives you something to rejoice in, something to talk about, and something to look forward to. He goes before you!

Saved Through Faith

Sinners are saved through faith in Christ (Eph. 2:8–9), and they bear witness of their faith through baptism (Mark 16:16; Acts 10:47). Some signs described in Mark 16:17–18 occurred during the apostolic period described in the book of Acts. They were the "credentials" of the apostles (Heb. 2:1–4; Rom. 15:19; 2 Cor. 12:12), so we must not assume that they belong to every believer today. It is foolish to tempt God by drinking poison or handling poisonous snakes, but it is not foolish to trust God when obedience to His will takes us into dangerous situations. Presumption can kill us, but faith can deliver us.

He appeared (9–18). This section summarizes the Lord's resurrection appearances. All to whom He appeared became witnesses of His resurrection (Acts 1:22), just as we should be today (Rom. 6:4; Phil. 3:10).

He ascended (19–20). The Servant is the Sovereign at the Father's right hand! He humbled Himself in obedience, and God exalted Him in glory (Phil. 2:5–11). But He is not idle, for He is working with His people as they take the gospel to every nation. What an encouragement to be a witness for your Lord!

LUKE

◆

Luke was a physician, probably a Greek (Col. 4:10–11, 14), the companion of Paul on some of his journeys. (Note the pronouns "we" and "us" in Acts 16:10; 20:5; 21:1; 27:1.) He wrote the gospel of Luke and the book of Acts (Luke 1:1–4; Acts 1:1–3), both of which are records of journeys: Christ's journey to Jerusalem (Luke 9:51) and Paul's journey to Rome.

Dr. Luke wrote with the Greeks in mind and presented Jesus Christ as the perfect Son of man, the compassionate Savior (Luke 19:10). He mentions women, children, and the poor often in his gospel; and *joy* and *rejoicing* are repeated many times. There is also an emphasis on prayer and on God's love for the whole world. Luke addressed both books to Theophilus ("lover of God"), a Roman believer, possibly an official, who needed grounding in the faith.

Luke's approach is simple. He records our Lord's birth and early life (chaps. 1–2); His baptism and temptation (3:1–4:13); His ministry in Galilee (4:14–9:17); His ministry en route to Jerusalem (9:18–19:27); and His final week of ministry in Jerusalem (19:28–24:53).

As you read the gospel of Luke, you will come to love the compassionate Son of man who cares for those in need and wants His message of salvation to be taken to the whole world.

LUKE 1

Serving (1–25). His disappointment at not having a son did not keep Zacharias from serving the Lord. Be faithful; you never know when God's angel may arrive. Zacharias had the faith to keep on praying; but when the answer came, he did not have the faith to accept it. He looked at his limitations rather than God's great power. Unbelief produces silence (Ps.

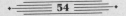

116:10; 2 Cor. 4:13); faith opens your mouth in praise to God.

Submitting (26–38). What an honor to be chosen to be the mother of the Messiah! Mary humbly submitted to the Lord because she had faith that He would keep His promise. Her decision would bring her sorrow and suffering, but she willingly yielded it. She was "blessed among women" because of the grace of God given to her (vv. 28, 30). All who trust Christ as their Savior are highly graced by the Lord (Eph. 1:6).

Jesus' Greatness	It was said of John the Baptist, "He will be great in the sight of the Lord" (Luke 1:15); but of Jesus it was said, "He will be great" (Luke 1:32). He is the great Prophet (Luke 7:16), the great God and Savior (Titus 2:13), the great High Priest (Heb. 4:14), and the great Shepherd of the sheep (Heb. 13:20).

"Do Not Be Afraid"	The encouraging phrase "Do not be afraid!" is found often in Luke's gospel, for the message of salvation replaces fear with joy. All kinds of people heard it: Zacharias (1:13), Mary (1:30), the shepherds (2:10), Peter (5:10), Jairus (8:50), and the disciples (12:7, 32).

Singing (39–80). A pregnant Jewish girl from Nazareth, engaged to marry a poor carpenter, what did Mary have to sing about? She sang about the Lord, what He did for *her* (vv. 46–49), for *all who fear Him* (vv. 50–53), and for *His people Israel* (vv. 54–55). God gives power to the weak, thrones to the lowly, and food to the hungry; but the strong, the rich, and the mighty go away empty.

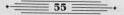

Zacharias praised God for what He would do for His people, Israel. It was the dawning of a new day (vv. 78–79) because the Messiah was about to be born. God keeps His promises and is faithful to His covenants.

LUKE 2

You cannot escape Jesus Christ.

His birth affected Caesar's politics (vv. 1–3), the ministry of the angels (vv. 8–15), and the activities of common men (vv. 15–20). In that day, shepherds were looked upon with disdain; but God singled them out to be the first human messengers of Messiah's birth. His coming touched worshipers (vv. 21–38) and even scholars (vv. 39–52).

The angels sang about Him, and He is still the theme of the greatest music. Luke wrote about Him, and He is still the subject of the greatest literature. The shepherds hastened to behold Him, and He is still at the center of the greatest art. Teachers listened to Him and marveled, and He is still the focal point for all truth and wisdom.

In His development, Jesus was perfectly balanced: intellectually (wisdom), physically (stature), spiritually (in favor with God), and socially (in favor with man); and He is still the greatest example for childhood and youth.

He alone is worthy of our worship!

Oh, come! Let us adore Him!

LUKE 3

Prophecy. God's message did not come to any of the "great leaders" of that day. It came to John the Baptist, the last and the greatest of God's prophets. John's ministry was foretold by the prophet Isaiah (vv. 4–6; Isa. 40:3–5). John was a prophet who was the subject of prophecy.

Ministry. John was privileged to prepare the nation for the Messiah and then present Him to them. John preached against sin and told the people to repent. He gave specific instructions to his converts on how to put their faith into practice. He was inspecting fruit (v. 8), getting to the root of sin (v. 9), and warning about wrath to come (vv. 7, 17). Would you accept that kind of ministry?

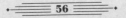

Mystery. The Son of God is baptized; the Spirit lights upon Him like a dove; and the Father speaks His approval from heaven. Never forget that all of the holy Trinity is involved in your salvation (Eph. 1:1–14).

History. The genealogy (vv. 23–38) is that of Mary whose father was Heli. Joseph was not the biological father of Jesus, though that was what people assumed (John 1:45; 6:42). The genealogy of Joseph is found in Matthew 1. It was unusual to pay attention to the genealogy of a woman, which shows Dr. Luke's concern for neglected people. Gentile history (v. 1) and Jewish history (vv. 23–38) are in the hands of almighty God, fulfilling His purposes.

LUKE 4

The Conqueror (1–13). You can be filled with the Spirit (v. 1) and obedient to God's will and still experience temptations and trials. Because He faced the enemy and conquered, Jesus can identify with you in your temptations and can help you win the victory (Heb. 2:17–18). It is not a sin to be tempted, for Jesus was tempted; but it is a sin to yield. Satan's promise is, "All will be yours" (v. 7); but in Jesus Christ, you already have all things (1 Cor. 3:21–23), and Satan can give you nothing.

The Preacher (14–30). The Spirit not only gives us victory, but He leads us (v. 14) and empowers us for service (v. 18). The text for our Lord's message was Isaiah 61:1-2. It describes what Jesus came to do and what He is still doing in lives today. The people in the synagogue wanted a comforting sermon, not a convicting sermon. When Jesus mentioned God's grace to the Gentiles (vv. 23–27), the people became angry and threw Him out! They forfeited His blessings because they rejected His word.

The Healer (31–44). Jesus fulfilled His commission (vv. 18–19) by bringing healing and deliverance to the poor and needy by the authority of His word. Had He not overcome the devil privately, Jesus could not have defeated him publicly. While the preaching of the Word was His major ministry (vv. 42–44), Jesus had compassion on the sick and healed them. We may not have the power to heal, but we can comfort and assist those who are needy; and we can do it in Jesus' name (Matt. 25:34–40).

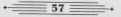

LUKE 5

Jesus responds to submission (1–11). If you had fished all night and caught nothing, would you be getting ready to go out fishing again? One reason Jesus called several fishermen to be His disciples was that they never quit! Peter may have thought he knew more about fishing than Jesus did, but he did what Jesus commanded; and the Lord honored his obedient faith. No failure is final if you come to the Lord for a new start.

Jesus responds to sickness (12–14). Lepers were not to approach people; but the man came to Jesus in desperation, and Jesus healed him. The offering Jesus referred to is described in Leviticus 14 and pictures the salvation work of the Lord. Ponder it.

Jesus responds to success (15–16). The crowds sought Him, but Jesus withdrew to pray and commune with the Father. He did not allow popularity to detour Him from the Father's will. Vance Havner said, "Success can feather our nest so comfortably that we forget how to fly."

Jesus responds to sinners (17–39). He forgave the paralytic, Matthew the publican, and Matthew's friends who trusted Him because He is the "friend of sinners" (Matt. 11:19). He could not forgive the scribes and Pharisees because they would not admit they were sick and in need of new clothes!

"They Forsook All"	Peter and his associates had met the Lord earlier (John 1:35–42), had gone with Him on His ministry through Galilee (Mark 1:16–20), but had returned to their fishing business. They now had the call to leave everything and follow the Lord as His apostles (Luke 5:9–11).

LUKE 6

True liberty (1–11). People who live only by "Is it lawful?" cannot understand our Lord's principle, "Is it loving?" The

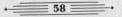

scribes and Pharisees had transformed the Sabbath from a day of blessing into a day of bondage, and Jesus deliberately healed on the Sabbath so He could challenge them. It is always right to do good and to meet human need (Mic. 6:8), for love fulfills the law (Rom. 13:8–10).

True values (12–26). In His ordination sermon for the apostles, Jesus emphasized the true spiritual values of life in contrast to the false values of the Pharisees (Matt. 23). Comfortable living is not always Christian living.

True love (27–45). Yes, God's people have their enemies, even as Jesus did; and we must be Christlike in the way we treat them. We must be giving and forgiving; and we must pray for them, not that God would destroy them but that He would change them. The best way to conquer an enemy is to make him a friend. Keep your heart right with God (v. 45) and the Lord will produce the good fruit in your life.

True obedience (46–49). True obedience is not just words but deeds, and it involves hearing the Word and doing it (1 Thess. 2:13). Judas knew the vocabulary, but he did not do the will of God; and when the storm came, his house fell.

LUKE 7

He did not deserve it (1–10). "I am not worthy" was the centurion's confession of humility; and his confession of faith was, "Say the word!" It is great faith when we trust Christ to work just by speaking the Word. We can never deserve His blessings, but we can ask for them in faith.

True Rest   *Christ's invitation to come to Him for rest (Matt. 11:28–30) precedes Luke 7:36–50. The sinful woman had heard that invitation and had come to Christ, and she found rest. She was ashamed of her past, but she was not ashamed of her Savior or of her tears.*

She did not expect it (11–17). Nobody knew that Jesus would arrive and break up the funeral! Never despair, because your Lord may surprise you at the last minute and do the impossible for you.

He did not understand it (18–35). When the Lord is not doing what you expect Him to do, tell Him about it and listen to His Word. You may feel that your ministry has failed, but you are not the judge. Let Jesus have the final word.

She could not hide it (36–50). The sinful woman trusted Christ and He saved her; now she wanted to express her love to Him. True faith cannot be hidden, and true faith shows itself in love and worship. Simon the Pharisee was blind: he could not see himself, the Lord, or the woman. He did not know the debt he owed!

LUKE 8

A multitude hearing Him (1–25). Jesus was not impressed by the crowds that followed Him, for He knew the spiritual condition of their hearts. The parable of the sower helps us examine our hearts to see how we respond to the Word. But it is not enough to hear the Word (vv. 8, 18); we must also obey it (v. 21) and trust it when the time of testing comes (vv. 22–25).

A multitude rejecting Him (26–39). The healing of the Gadarene demoniacs (Matt. 8:28) should have endeared Jesus to the people, but the citizens were concerned more about pigs and money than about people and mercy. The man who begged to go with Jesus was the sanest one of all!

A multitude welcoming Him (40). This was on the other side of the Sea of Galilee, near Capernaum. Why did they welcome Him? Probably not because of their love for Him, but because they had seen many of His miracles and wanted Him to meet their needs. If Jesus were coming today, would you welcome Him? Why?

A multitude thronging Him (41–56). The people wanted to get next to Jesus so He could help them; but though they thronged Him, they did not have the touch of faith that the poor sick woman had. Being in the crowd is no assurance of receiving the blessing. Sometimes God has to get you away from the crowd before He can meet the need (v. 51).

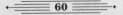

LUKE 9

Christ equips us (1-6). He will never send us out to do a task without first giving us what we need. We are prone to trust what we have, but we should trust in Him alone. If we are in His will, we will have His supply.

Christ enables us (7-17). How could twelve men feed five thousand people? Only through the enabling of the Lord, for He did the miracle: they only distributed the blessing. Christ is looking for clean empty hands that He can fill.

Christ encourages us (18-36). If you confess Christ as Son of God and Savior, and take up your cross and follow Him, He will reveal to you His kingdom and His glory. When you experience the glory of God, the demands of discipleship become blessings that carry you along in joyful obedience.

Christ endures us (37-62). What strange words from the lips of Jesus: "How long shall I be with you and bear with you?" (v. 41). He must bear with our unbelief and failure (vv. 37-42), our spiritual blindness (vv. 43-45), our pride (vv. 46-48), our lack of love (vv. 49-56), and our lack of dedication (vv. 57-62). Is Jesus blessing you—or bearing with you?

LUKE 10

The chapter asks four questions by way of personal inventory.

What makes you serve (1-16)? Jesus was not limited to the Twelve; seventy others obeyed Him and helped to reap the harvest. But the laborers are still few, and Luke 9:57-62 tells why. The ministry is difficult and dangerous, but it is also very rewarding. Are you obedient to His call?

What makes you rejoice (17-24)? When the disciples rejoiced over their successful ministry, Jesus told them to rejoice because they were the citizens of heaven. After all, their work might not always be successful; but their salvation would never change. Jesus rejoiced because the Father's will was being accomplished in their lives. What brings joy to your heart?

What makes you pause (25-37)? It is not difficult to discuss neighborliness in the abstract, but it costs something to be a

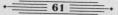

real neighbor. Do you pause to help when you see injustice and hurt, or like the priest and the Levite, do you look for an escape? You are never more Christlike than when you feel another's hurt and seek to help.

What makes you listen (38–42)? Here is the basis for all ministry, taking time to sit at the feet of Jesus and hear His Word. It is important to serve the Lord and serve others, but it is even more important to delight your Lord by spending time with Him. Are you so busy serving Him that you have no time to love Him and listen to Him?

Serving Him

Faithful to my Lord's commands,
I still would choose the better part;
Serve with careful Martha's hands
And loving Mary's heart.

Charles Wesley

❝ *Justice seeks out the merits of the case, but pity only regards the need.* **❞**

Bernard of Clairvaux

LUKE 11

His generosity (1–13). If Jesus, John the Baptist, and the Twelve all needed to pray, how much more do *we* need to pray! We must put God's concerns first (vv. 2–4), because prayer is based on *sonship*, not friendship. God is a loving Father, not a grouchy neighbor; He gives us what we need. He neither slumbers nor sleeps; and He doesn't become irritated when we ask for help (James 1:5).

His authority (14–36). More dangerous than open hostility (vv. 14–22) is attempted neutrality (vv. 23–26), for an empty life is an opportunity for Satan to move in and take over. The only sign we need is the "sign of Jonah," our Lord's resurrection from the dead (Acts 2:22–36). Jesus has won the victory over the prince of darkness. Obey Satan and you let in darkness rather than light, and soon you will not be able to distinguish between them (Matt. 6:22–23).

His honesty (37–54). He was a guest in the home, but Jesus did not flatter His host or the other guests by avoiding the truth. He exposed their hypocrisy and condemned them for their sins (Matt. 23). They defiled people (v. 44), burdened them (v. 46), and locked the door on them (v. 52), all the while posing as holy men of God. Instead of taking the opportunity of repenting and being forgiven, they opposed Jesus and attacked Him. What fools!

> **❝***Prayer is a mighty instrument, not for getting man's will done in Heaven, but for getting God's will done in earth.***❞**
>
> Robert Law

LUKE 12

A fearful heart (1–12). When you fear people, you start to hide things, and this leads to hypocrisy. You fail to confess Christ openly and depend on the Holy Spirit (vv. 8–12), and this silences your witness. When you fear God alone, you need fear no one else; and you can boldly witness for Christ. You are important to God and precious in His sight, so never fear what people can say or do.

A greedy heart (13–21). Imagine being so greedy that you would interrupt a sermon to ask for help to get more money! The weeds were certainly growing in that man's heart (Matt. 13:22). We all need a certain amount of money to live, but money is not a guarantee of security. If anything, it creates a *false* confidence that leads to foolishness.

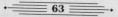

A divided heart (22–34). The word translated "worry" (v. 22) means "to be pulled apart," and that is what worry does to you. If your heart is centered on Christ and trusting wholly in Him (v. 31), you will have a united heart that fears God alone (Ps. 86:11). If your treasures are heavenly, you need not worry; no enemy can take them!

A cold heart (35–59). We are God's servants, and He expects us to be faithfully doing our work when Jesus Christ returns. But when we stop looking for His coming, loving it (2 Tim. 4:8), and longing for it (Rev. 22:20), our hearts get cold, and we get worldly. The Lord will deal with careless servants when He returns, so we had better be ready.

LUKE 13

Tragedy (1–9). How easy it is to ask questions about others' tragedies and fail to learn the lessons they teach! The big question is not "Why do people die in tragic and seemingly meaningless ways?" but "Why does God keep me alive?" Am I really worth it? Am I bearing fruit or just taking up space?

Hypocrisy (10–17). The ruler of the synagogue was a hypocrite because he treated animals better than he treated people. Suppose the woman did come to the synagogue on another day. Could he have healed her? Of course not! We wonder how many needy people come to church meetings looking for love and help and go away disappointed.

> **"**Yesterday is a canceled check. Tomorrow is a promissory note. Today is the only cash you have, so invest it wisely.**"**

Opportunity (18–35). God's kingdom is at work in this world, but many people fail to take advantage of their opportunities. Instead of entering the kingdom, some people only ask questions about it. Salvation is not a theory to discuss; it is a miracle to experience. No wonder Jesus wept when He saw sinners passing by their opportunities to be saved! Do not wait for opportunities to come; they are already here.

LUKE 14

Do I exploit people (1–14)? When we eat together, it should be a time of loving fellowship and joyful gratitude to God; but the Pharisees turned tables into traps and exploited people. They used a man with a handicapping condition in trying to catch Jesus; they went to feasts only to receive honors; and they invited to their feasts only people who would return the favor. Hospitality is ministry only if our motive is to help others and glorify God.

Do I invite people (15–24)? Salvation is a feast, not a funeral (5:33–39); and God wants His house filled. As His servants, we have the privilege to tell the world, "Come, for all things are now ready!" (v. 17). Even if some reject the invitation, keep sharing it. Those who think they are the least worthy are the ones He wants to have at His feast.

Do I follow people (25–35)? It is easy to be part of the crowd and follow a popular Jesus, but that is not true discipleship. He calls you away from the crowd to take up your cross and follow Him. When it comes to winning the lost, God wants His house filled; but when it comes to discipleship, Christ thins out the ranks and wants only those who will die to self and live for Him.

LUKE 15

These parables are Christ's defense of His ministry, explaining why He fellowshiped with sinners and even ate with them.

He saw what they were. They were sheep that had gone astray and needed a shepherd to bring them home. They were lost coins, stamped with the image of God, needing to get back into circulation again. They were disobedient sons who were wasting their inheritance and needed to come home to the Father.

He saw how they got that way. Sheep are foolish animals and naturally go astray, but the spiritual shepherds in Israel

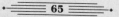

had not faithfully ministered to them (Jer. 23; Ezek. 34). The woman lost the coin because of carelessness, and the son was lost because of his willfulness. The father did not search for the boy but let him learn his lessons the hard way and discover how good it was back home. (See Rom. 2:4.)

He saw what they could be. Jesus always saw the potential in people. The sheep could be brought back to the flock and bring joy to the shepherd; the coin could be found; and the son could return home and lovingly serve his father. There is hope for every sinner because Jesus welcomes everyone.

LUKE 16

The subject is money, and the object is to teach us the proper place of money in life.

We can waste money (1). Stewards should use wealth for their masters' good and not for their own pleasure (1 Cor. 4:2). God wants us to *enjoy* His gifts (1 Tim. 6:17), but He also wants us to *employ* them wisely.

We can serve God with money (2–9). The man had a rude awakening: he had to give an account of his stewardship (Rom. 14:10–12; 2 Cor. 5:10). Then he learned to be wise and to invest wealth in people and in the future. We do not "buy" friends, but we can make friends for the Lord by the wise use of money. Will people welcome you to heaven because your stewardship made it possible for them to hear the gospel and be saved?

66*Make all you can, save all you can, give all you can.*99

John Wesley

66*Money is a wonderful servant, a terrible master, and an abominable god.*99

We can try to serve God and money (10–18). The Pharisees tried it but it cannot be done. How can you serve both righteousness and unrighteousness, what is greatest and what is least, what God honors and what He abominates? The world measures people by how much they get, but God measures them by how much they give.

We can let money be our god (19–31). The rich man did not go to Hades because he was rich; he went there because riches were his god. Abraham was a wealthy man, and yet he was in paradise. Money can help send people to heaven (v. 9), or it can help send people to hell.

LUKE 17

Faith is like a seed: it seems small and weak, but it has life in it; and if it is cultivated, it will grow and release power. We need faith for many areas of life.

Faith to forgive (1–4). When people sin repeatedly, giving up on them is easy; but we must forgive them and trust God to work in their lives. We must be stepping stones and not stumbling blocks.

Faith to serve (5–10). It takes faith to do your duty, whether tending a field or a flock or preparing a meal. It takes faith to do the extraordinary, like moving a mountain.

Faith to pray (11–19). The ten men believed that Jesus could help them, and He did. The Samaritan not only brought joy to Christ's heart but received salvation from His hand: "Your faith has saved you!" When God answers your prayers, be sure to tell Him "thank You!"

Faith to be ready when He comes (20–37). The important thing is not to set dates but to be ready when He comes, for true faith leads to faithfulness. To *look around* at the increase in sin will discourage you, and to *look back* (as did Lot's wife) may destroy you, so *look up* and eagerly expect the Lord's return today!

LUKE 18

Confident prayer (1–8). If an unjust judge helps a poor widow, how much more will a loving Father meet the needs of His children? We have open access into His treasury (Rom.

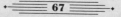

5:2) and can claim His gracious promises (Luke 11:9–10), so we ought to pray with faith and confidence. No need to argue—just come!

Arrogant prayer (9–17). True prayer should humble us and make us love others more. We should be like children coming to a Father and not like attorneys bringing an indictment. If prayer doesn't bless the one praying, it isn't likely to help anybody else.

Ignorant prayer (18–34). Although the young man had many good qualities, one of them was not spiritual understanding. He did not really see himself, Jesus, or the peril he was in because of his riches. The publican went away justified (v. 14) while the young man went away sorrowful (v. 23). What happens at the close of your prayers?

Persistent prayer (35–43). The blind man was not to be stopped! He had his great opportunity, and he would not let it pass. Our Lord stopped, looked, listened—and healed! Jesus is not too busy to hear you. Just be sure you are in earnest when you pray.

> **“**The revelation of our spiritual standing is what we ask in prayer; sometimes what we ask is an insult to God; we ask with our eyes on the possibilities or on ourselves, not on Jesus Christ.**”**
>
> Oswald Chambers

LUKE 19

The day of salvation (1–10). Verse 10 is illustrated in the experience of Zacchaeus: Jesus *came* to him, *sought* him, and *saved* him. Though He was surrounded by a great crowd of people, Jesus took time for individuals, and He even saw a man in a tree! He is still the seeking Savior, but now He uses *your* eyes and lips.

The day of evaluation (11–27). There are three possible relationships with the King. You can reject His rule and be an

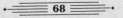

enemy, but that leads to judgment. You can accept His rule and be unfaithful, but that leads to loss of reward. Or you can accept His rule, do His will faithfully, and receive His reward. You are not to *protect* what He gives you but to *invest* it for His glory.

The day of visitation (28–43). What a tragedy that the Jewish nation did not know their own King when He came to them! But when He comes again, "will He really find faith on the earth" (18:8)? Our Lord wept, for He saw the terrible judgment that was coming to the city and the people.

God Seeks . . .	*What is God looking for? He is seeking the lost (Luke 19:10), worshipers (John 4:23), fruit in our lives (Luke 13:7), and faithful servants (Ezek. 22:30). Has He found you?*

LUKE 20

In spite of their evasive and hypocritical reply, the leaders *could not escape the past* (vv. 1–8). They had rejected the ministry of John the Baptist, and that led to their refusal to trust Jesus Christ. You may forget your decisions, but they will not forget you. You may even try to bury them, but they will be resurrected to accuse you.

❝Truth is incontrovertible. Panic may resent it; ignorance may deride it; malice may distort it; but there it is.**❞**

Sir Winston Churchill

Nor could they *escape future judgment* (vv. 9–19). They would reject the Son and the Stone, and that would bring about their ruin. Christ either saves you or judges you; there is no middle ground.

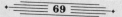

The leaders even failed to *escape present responsibility* (vv. 20–47). In asking Jesus trick questions, they hoped He would say something they could accuse; but His answers only exposed their folly and increased their guilt. They were fighting a losing battle and would not surrender.

LUKE 21

Maintaining the temple (1–4). Many of the religious leaders were corrupt, but the temple was still the place where God put His name and where sincere people could worship Him. Jesus did not criticize the people for supporting the temple ministry (Matt. 23:1–3), but He did notice *what* they gave. The *proportion*, not the portion, is important. Those who give "the widow's mite" give their all, not their least.

Destroying the temple (5–36). This is Luke's version of the Olivet Discourse found also in Matthew 24—25 and Mark 13. He is the only gospel writer who deals with our Lord's prediction of the fall of Jerusalem, which occurred in A.D. 70 (vv. 20–24). The rest of his report describes events in the last days before the return of Jesus Christ to earth. It will be a time of testing and testimony, oppression and opportunity, vengeance and victory.

Ministering in the temple (37–38). As a boy of twelve, Jesus discussed the Word in the temple (2:41–50); and He spent the last week before His death teaching the Word in His Father's house. He was hated by the religious leaders, and the temple was a den of thieves; but needy people were there, and Jesus taught them. He was quick to seize the opportunity, and the people were glad to hear Him.

LUKE 22

Satan in the temple (1–6). Judas was energized by Satan when he made his agreement with the religious leaders. Satan is a liar and murderer (John 8:44), and he helped Judas with his deception. But Satan deceived Judas as well, and the former disciple ended up a suicide. It is dangerous to make deals with the devil.

Satan in the Upper Room (7–38). Satan already controlled Judas, but he had to ask for permission to "sift" the disciples

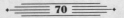

and to tempt Peter (Job 1:12; 2:6). Satan is not all-powerful and must obey the limits set by the Lord (1 Cor. 10:13). The apostles had experienced some great blessings that evening, but danger was very near. Be on your guard when you have had a rich spiritual experience, for Satan is about to attack. And especially beware when you are trying to decide who is the greatest!

Satan in the Garden (39–53). Jesus said to those who had come to arrest Him, "But this is your hour, and the power of darkness" (v. 53). Because He had prayed and was yielded to the Father's will, Jesus was prepared for the arrest, but the disciples were not. If ever the work of Christ appeared to be ruined, it was in the garden; *but that was when Jesus was doing His very best in the Father's will.*

Satan in the courts (54–71). Satan was in the courtyard to sift Peter and in the council chamber to lead the men astray. His victory over Peter was only temporary, for the apostle wept, repented, and was restored. His victory over the religious leaders was complete, for he blinded their eyes to the truth (2 Cor. 4:3–6) and they condemned their own Messiah.

LUKE 23

Pilate wanted to get rid of Jesus as quickly and as easily as possible, but you cannot avoid making serious decisions about Him. Pilate ended up condemning an innocent Man, releasing a guilty man, and making friends with a wicked man. What a record for a Roman ruler whose responsibility it was to uphold the law and give people justice!

Herod wanted to see Jesus do a miracle! The evil king would make the Son of God into a court entertainer. Jesus performed no miracle; He spoke no word. Herod had silenced God's voice, and there was nothing left for him but divine judgment.

Barabbas deserved to die but was set free because Jesus took his place. Did Barabbas go to Calvary and look at the Man who died for him? Probably not. He was glad to be free from the sentence of death so he could return to his old ways. He was free but still in the bondage of sin.

*And for those people—and many more—*Jesus prayed, "Father, forgive them, for they do not know what they do" (v. 34). What grace!

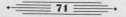

The thief exercised great faith when he asked Jesus to remember him, for Jesus did not look like He was able to save anybody.

Joseph exercised great courage when he openly took our Lord's body from the cross. He defiled himself for Passover week, but it made no difference: he had met the Lamb of God, and that was all that mattered.

LUKE 24

Forgetting His word (1–12). The stone was rolled away, the body of Jesus was gone, and the women were perplexed. Why? Because they had forgotten His word. Today, angels do not come to remind us of His word; the Holy Spirit has that ministry (John 14:26). Yield to the Spirit and let Him remind you of the promises that will encourage your heart.

Learning the Word (13–35). Those two men could have walked and talked for days and never gotten rid of their disappointment. Why? Because they lacked the key that unlocks the Old Testament: Messiah must suffer and die before entering His glory. Their hearts burned as they heard Him teach the Scriptures; and soon, the mourners became missionaries and shared the good news with others. Do you allow the Holy Spirit to teach you (John 16:13–15)?

Receiving the Word (36–45). Their hearts were troubled, frightened, and doubtful; yet the Lord lovingly reassured them with His word. We today cannot see or feel His body, but we have the Holy Spirit to make Him real to us from the Scriptures. When your heart is troubled or frightened, see Jesus in the Word (John 14:1–6). When your faith is weak, see Jesus in the Word (Rom. 10:17). The first step toward peace is receiving the Word.

Sharing the Word (46–53). God opens our eyes (v. 31) and opens our understanding (v. 45) so that when He opens the Scriptures to us (vv. 27, 32), we may open our mouths and tell others about Him (v. 48). Jesus gives us the commission, the power, and the message. There is no reason to be silent! When we experience joyful worship (vv. 52–53), we will have little problem giving the world a joyful witness.

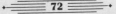

JOHN

John had two purposes in mind when he wrote his gospel: to prove that Jesus Christ is the Son of God, and to invite people to believe in Him and be saved (20:30–31). His evidence for the deity of Jesus Christ is threefold: (1) the miracles He performed; (2) the words He spoke; and (3) the testimony of witnesses who knew Him.

As you read the gospel of John, you will hear Jesus speak (7:46), see Him act in power, and watch people respond to what He says and does. Seven witnesses declare that He is the Son of God: John the Baptist (1:34), Nathanael (1:49), Peter (6:69), a man who had been blind (9:35–38), Martha (11:27), Thomas (20:28), and the apostle John (20:31). Jesus also declared His deity (5:25; 10:36).

Matthew wrote for the Jews, Mark for the Romans, and Luke for the Greeks. However, John had the whole world in mind when he wrote and frequently used the word *world*. But he alludes to the Old Testament over one hundred times, showing that he was mindful of his Jewish readers.

The invitation in the synoptic Gospels is, "Come and hear!" But in the Gospel of John, the invitation is also, "Come and see!" There are sixty-seven references in the book to seeing and fifty-eight to hearing. His *works* and His *words* prove that Jesus is indeed the Son of God.

After the introduction (1:1–18), John describes the ministry of Christ to His people (1:19—12:50), to His disciples (chaps. 13—17), and then to the whole world (chaps. 18—21). In the first section, He is the Miracle Worker; in the second, the Teacher; and in the third, the Victor. Of course, throughout the book, Jesus is seen as Savior and Lord.

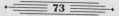

JOHN 1

The Creator came (1–14). Compare this passage with Genesis 1 and note the emphasis on *light* and *life*. Moses wrote about the old creation, but John wrote about the new creation (2 Cor. 5:17). Jesus is the creative Word and the living Word who reveals the Father to us. In His many miracles, Jesus showed His power as Creator. He is a faithful Creator, and you can trust your life to Him (1 Pet. 4:19).

The Savior came (15–34). He came with grace and truth, not law and judgment. He revealed the Father and gave the Holy Spirit to those who trusted Him. He is the Lamb of God who alone can take away sins. The blood of lambs *covered* the sins of *the Jews,* but the blood of Christ *takes away* the sins of *the whole world* (v. 29; 4:42).

The Master came (35–51). Jesus called a few men to follow Him, and He transformed their lives and used them to transform the lives of others. Simon's new name (Peter, meaning "a stone") symbolized a new beginning in his life. He became a part of the new creation, sharing in the fullness of grace (v. 16). Jesus calls each one individually and uses different approaches, but the same Master calls. Have you heeded His call?

Images of Jesus

John pictures our Lord's death as the slaying of the lamb (1:29), the destroying of a temple (2:19), the lifting up of a serpent (3:14), the voluntary death of a shepherd (10:11–18), and the planting of a seed (12:20–25).

The King came (49). Jesus came to His own creation and everything in creation obeyed Him; but His own people did not receive Him (v. 11; 12:37–41). During His trial before Pilate, His kingship was the paramount issue (18:33—19:22); and it is still the issue today. Who is the king of *your* life?

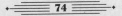

JOHN 2

Look at Jesus!

He is joyous (1–12). A Jewish wedding is a joyful event, and Jesus was very much at home there. He was "a man of sorrows" (Isa. 53:3), but He also experienced great joy (Luke 10:21); and He can share the joys and sorrows (chap. 11) of our lives. The joy the world offers will eventually fail, but the joy He supplies goes on forever. Be sure to invite Him, and be sure to obey what He says.

He is righteous (13–17). The other gospels record His cleansing of the temple at the close of His ministry, but John tells us He started His ministry by cleansing the temple. Judgment begins at the house of God (1 Pet. 4:17). The temple was then "a house of merchandise" (v. 16); three years later, it was a "den of thieves" (Matt. 21:13). Outward reformation without inward renewal is a temporary thing.

He is victorious (18–25). The Jews repeatedly asked Him for a sign (1 Cor. 1:22) and then rejected the evidence He provided (12:37–41). His resurrection was the greatest proof of His deity (Matt. 12:38–40), but the Jews did not understand what He was talking about (8:42–45). They would destroy the temple by crucifying Him, but He would triumph over them in His resurrection.

◆────────────────────

Understanding Divine Truths

In his gospel, John points out that unsaved people did not understand what Jesus taught. When He used symbolic language to illustrate a spiritual truth, they took it literally. That was true when He spoke about the temple (2: 18–22), the new birth (3:1–9), living water (4:7–15), and eating His flesh and drinking His blood (6:51–52). Apart from the Spirit, you cannot understand His Word (1 Cor. 2:6–16).

Miraculous Works	Out of the many miracles Jesus performed, John selected seven to reveal His glory and prove His deity: turning water into wine (2:1–11); healing the nobleman's son (4:46–54); healing the man sick for thirty-eight years (chap. 5); feeding the five thousand (6:1–14); walking on the stormy sea (6:15–21); restoring sight to a man born blind (chap. 9); and raising Lazarus from the dead (chap. 11). The catch of fish (chap. 21), was performed after His resurrection.

JOHN 3

A birth from above (1–9). In our first birth, we are "born of the flesh" and "born of water"; but in our second birth, we are "born from above [again]" and "born of the Spirit." Our first birth leads to death, but our second birth brings eternal life. The new birth is a new beginning that results in "newness of life" (Rom. 6:4).

A Savior from above (10–21). Jesus is the Son of God come down from heaven. He is the serpent Moses wrote about (Num. 21:4–9); He is the Father's love gift (v. 16); He is the Light in a dark world (v. 19). Like the serpent, He was lifted up, and He died on a cross for the sins of the world. All who look to Him by faith receive eternal life.

A witness from above (22–36). John's ministry was given to him from heaven (v. 27). His task was to bear witness to Jesus (1:6–8). Jesus is the Word, and John was only a voice proclaiming the Word (1:23). Jesus is the Bridegroom, but John was only the best man. John did no miracles, but his witness was used to win people to Christ, even after he was dead (10:40–42). Can you honestly say, "He must increase, but I must decrease" (v. 30)?

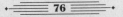

Nicodemus
> Nicodemus came to Jesus by night, but he finally came out into the light and identified with the Lord Jesus (19:38–42). Nicodemus gave Jesus an honest hearing (7:45–52), examined the Word, and became a believer.

JOHN 4

Thirst (1–26). Because Jesus was truly human, He experienced weariness, hunger, and thirst, but His deepest desire was for the salvation of the sinful woman. He forgot His physical needs and concentrated on her spiritual needs. Patiently He revealed Himself to her: "a Jew" (v. 9), "greater than Jacob" (v. 12), "a prophet" (v. 19), "Messiah" (vv. 25, 29). She believed in Him, and her life was so changed that she immediately shared the good news with others (20:30–31).

Hunger (27–42). The will of God should be food that nourishes us, not medicine that upsets us. The disciples were satisfied with material food, but Jesus wanted the satisfying spiritual food from God. The will of God gives us the strength we need to do our job in the great harvest all around us.

Health (43–54). Salvation is to the inner person what health is to the body. The boy would have died had Jesus not intervened and given him health. The father *heard* (v. 47), *believed* (v. 50), and *knew* (v. 53), which is a normal Christian experience.

Jesus won the woman; the woman won many Samaritans; and the father won his whole household. Are you busy in the harvest?

JOHN 5

Works (vv. 1–21). The Father "broke" His Sabbath rest to help two sinners (Gen. 3:8ff.), and Jesus followed His example. In the world of nature, the Father is healing bodies, multiplying food, turning water into wine, and so forth; but He takes

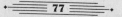

longer to do those things. Our Lord's miracles are the Father's works done instantly. Whether instantly or gradually, they are wonderful works of God.

Wrath (22, 24–30). Today, Jesus is the Savior; tomorrow, He will be the Judge (Rev. 20:11–15). Even death cannot keep lost sinners from the judgment, for He will raise them from the dead. There is no escape, except faith in Jesus Christ (5:24).

Worship (23). If you worship God the Father, you must also worship the Son; and if you dishonor the Son, you dishonor the Father. Those who claim to worship God but ignore the Son are not even worshiping God! They are only fooling themselves.

Witness (31–47). How can anyone deny that Jesus is the Son of God when so many witnesses affirm that He is: John the Baptist (vv. 31–35), the miracles (v. 36), the Father (v. 37; Mark 1:11), and the Scriptures (vv. 38–39)? But when people believe on Him, they have the witness within themselves (vv. 39–47; 1 John 5:9–13).

JOHN 6

The disciples faced three tests because of the great crowds that followed Jesus.

Feeding the multitude (1–14). Philip thought the answer was money, but Andrew saw the answer in a lad with a lunch. When you face a seemingly unsolvable problem, claim the promise of verse 6, give what you have to Jesus, and let Him tell you what to do.

Leaving the multitude (15–21). This incident occurred at the high point of our Lord's popularity. The disciples (especially Judas) would have welcomed a kingdom, so Jesus sent them away into a storm. They went from popularity to peril, but they were safer in the storm than with the multitude; and Jesus came to them and met their needs (Isa. 43:2). Can you obey His will even when you disagree with Him?

Losing the multitude (22–71). People want the Lord to meet their physical needs but not their spiritual needs. The manna (Exod. 16) came only to the Jews and *sustained* physical life, but Jesus came for the whole world and *gives* eternal life. Just as you take food into your body, so you take Christ into your life; and He becomes one with you. The disciples had opportunity to follow the crowd, but they remained with Jesus.

JOHN 7

How the world thinks (1–9). Because He was doing the Father's will, Jesus lived on a divine timetable (v. 30; 2:4; 8:20; 13:1), and so should we (Ps. 31:14–15). The world does not understand this and will give you advice contrary to God's will. Live on God's schedule and you will always have God's help.

How the world decides (10–36). This discussion reveals the confusion and unbelief of the people. Some were for Him because of His miracles, while others opposed Him because He broke the Sabbath laws. Some waited to see what their leaders would do (v. 26), and their leaders wanted to kill Him. They were judging by appearances (v. 24) and going astray.

What the world needs (37–53). One ritual during the Feast of Tabernacles was the pouring out of water in the temple. It was a reminder that God gave Israel water in the wilderness. Water for drinking pictures the Holy Spirit who is given to those who trust Christ. The world is thirsty and can find its thirst quenched only by coming to Christ.

Life	Life *is a key theme in John's gospel; he uses the word nearly fifty times. Jesus is the life (14:6), the light of life (1:4; 8:12), and the bread of life (6:48); and He gives the water of life (7:37–39). Jesus laid down His life so that we might have life (10:14–18, 27–30).*

JOHN 8

Condemnation (1–11). The woman was guilty, but where was the man? Both of them deserved to die (Lev. 20:10). It was a trap and Jesus knew it, but He ended up trapping the trap-

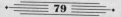

pers. Did He write on the ground to remind them that He had written the Law (Exod. 31:18) or to refer them to Jeremiah 17:13 (see Luke 10:20)? Here is our wonderful assurance: "There is therefore now no condemnation to those who are in Christ Jesus" (Rom. 8:1).

Illumination (12–29). The religious leaders did not know where they were going or where He was going because they were in the dark spiritually. They had the light of the Law (v. 5; Prov. 6:23) and of conscience (v. 9), but they did not have the light of life. Consequently, they did not know the Father or understand what Jesus taught them.

Liberation (30–59). The people were in bondage to Rome and to the Law of Moses, yet they said they were free! In verse 35, Jesus may have been referring to Isaac and Ishmael (Gen. 21:8–21), since the Jews had mentioned Abraham (v. 33). The Son makes you free (v. 36), so trust Him and follow Him. His truth makes you free (v. 32), so study it, believe it, and obey it. Satan imposes slavery that seems like freedom (2 Pet. 2:19); Jesus gives you a yoke that sets you free (Matt. 11:28–30).

Whose Child Are You?

There is no record that Jesus ever called the publicans and sinners "children of the devil." He reserved that title for the hypocritical Pharisees. By nature, we are all "children of wrath"; and by choice, we become "children of disobedience" (Eph. 2:1–3). When you receive Jesus Christ, you become a child of God (John 1:12–13). But if you reject Christ and have a false righteousness (Rom. 9:30—10:13), you are in danger of becoming a "child of the devil," for Satan is an imitator (2 Cor. 11:13–15). If Satan becomes your father, hell will be your home.

JOHN 9

Irritation (1–12). By putting clay on the man's eyes, Jesus encouraged him to obey and wash on the Sabbath. Sometimes the Lord irritates us before He illuminates us. His power is so great that He can use common things like dirt and water to produce a miracle. The man could hear but not see, and the Word produced faith (Rom. 10:17).

Interrogation (13–34). The man was questioned by the neighbors (v. 10) and by the Pharisees (vv. 15, 19, 26). Instead of seeking the truth and the freedom it brings (8:32), the Pharisees denied the truth and ended up in worse bondage. If we ask questions sincerely, with a willingness to obey, the Lord will lead us to the truth (7:17). If we are not honest with God, He will never show us His light.

Identification (35–41). The Pharisees were false shepherds who threw the man out, but Jesus the Good Shepherd took him in! The man knew that He was "a Man called Jesus" (v. 11), "a prophet" (v. 17), and "a Man of God" (v. 33); but he needed to learn that He is "the Son of God" (v. 35). He believed and was saved. Beware a spiritual experience that comes short of true salvation.

JOHN 10

God's people are His flock (Ps. 100:3; Acts 20:28), and they must beware strangers (v. 5), thieves (vv. 1, 10), and hirelings (v. 12). Jesus is the Good Shepherd who knows His sheep (vv. 14–15) and speaks to them (v. 27), so He is not like the strangers. He protects the sheep (vv. 28–29), so He is not like the thieves; and He gives His life for the sheep, so He is not like the hirelings who run away from danger (vv. 11–13).

When you trust the Good Shepherd, He leads you out of the wrong fold and into the right flock (vv. 3–4, 16). He goes before you and leads you by His Word (v. 4), and He leads you in and out to find spiritual nourishment (v. 9).

There are many churches but only "one flock and one shepherd" (v. 16). Is the Lord using you to bring the "other sheep" to Him?

In the Good Shepherd's Flock

Why does the Lord compare His people to sheep? They are prone to wander (Isa. 53:6) and need a shepherd to guide them. Sheep are clean animals (1 Pet. 2:25; 2 Pet. 2:20–22) and were used for sacrifices (Rom. 8:36; 12:1). They flock together (Acts 4:32) and are useful because they produce milk, lambs, and wool. The Good Shepherd knows His sheep intimately and calls them by name. He protects them and provides for them (Ps. 23). How wonderful to be one of His sheep!

JOHN 11

This experience was difficult for the Bethany family, but look at it in the light of God's love (vv. 3, 5, 36).

Love hears (1–3). The sisters sent their message to the Lord because they knew He was concerned about them. God's love keeps His ears open to our cries (Ps. 34:12–16).

Love waits (4–6). We think that love must act immediately, but sometimes delay brings a greater blessing. "God's delays are not God's denials." Jesus gave them a promise to encourage them while they waited (v. 4). The promise seemed to have failed, but Jesus knew what He was doing.

Love risks (7–16). It was dangerous for Jesus to return to Judea, but He went just the same. The raising of Lazarus helped to precipitate the plans that led to His death (vv. 45–57).

Love comforts (17–32). Jesus came to the sisters, listened to them, and assured them with His word. He cannot really help us until we move from "Lord, if . . ." (vv. 21, 32) to "Yes, Lord, I believe" (v. 27).

Love weeps (33–37). Jesus identifies with our sorrows (Heb.

4:15–16). He knew He would raise Lazarus from the dead, but He still wept with the sisters and their friends.

Love serves (38–44). We today are not able to raise the dead, but we can serve others as they go through the valley (Rom. 12:15). A loving heart will always find a way to bear others' burdens (Gal. 6:2).

> **❝**If God is at work week by week raising men from the dead, there will always be people coming to see how it is done. You cannot find an empty church that has conversion for its leading feature. Do you want to know how to fill empty chapels? Here is the answer: Get your Lazarus.**❞**
>
> Samuel Chadwick, Methodist evangelist and educator (1860–1932)

JOHN 12

Fragrance (1–11). What would your plans be if you knew you had only six days to live? Jesus took time to visit dear friends and fellowship with them. Mary's adoration not only revealed her love, but it brought joy to His heart, exposed Judas's sin, and gave the church an example to follow. Are the places where you go filled with Christ's fragrance because of you (2 Cor. 2:15–16)?

Festival (12–19). Jesus took advantage of the large Passover crowd to present Himself as King (Zech. 9:9). He was forcing the Jewish leaders to act, for it was the Father's will that Jesus die on Passover. The crowd did not stay with Him. It is easier to shout in a parade than stand at a cross.

Fruitfulness (20–36). Jesus looked upon His death as an opportunity to glorify God (vv. 23, 28). Do you take that attitude when you face a time of trial? He saw Himself as a seed that

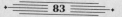

would die and produce fruit and as a conqueror who would defeat Satan (v. 31; Col. 2:14–15). The Cross would open the way of salvation for both Jews and Gentiles (v. 32).

Faithlessness (37–50). In His words and works, Jesus showed Israel the light, but they chose to walk in darkness. The praise of men meant more to them than the praise of God (5:44). Be careful what you do with His words because you will hear them again when you see the Savior (v. 48).

JOHN 13

What Jesus knew (1–11). Because of what Jesus knew, He did what He did: He washed the disciples' feet. Jesus knew where He came from and where He was going. He knew that the Father had given Him all things (3:35). If you have all things in your hand, you will have no problem picking up a towel (1 Cor. 3:21–23). Jesus taught them a lesson in fellowship and in keeping themselves clean before the Lord (1 John 1:5—2:1).

What the disciples knew (12–20). Jesus taught them a second lesson: true happiness comes from humble service. Jesus gave them an example that we must follow today (Phil. 2:1–11). Alas, soon after this lesson, the disciples began to argue over who was the greatest (Luke 22:24–30).

The Holy Spirit	*The Holy Spirit is the Father's gift to you, a gift that will never be taken back (John 14:16). The Spirit is a person, like the Father and the Son, and is God; and He dwells in God's people (14:17). He enables you to witness for Christ (15:26–27; Acts 1:8) and through your witness convicts the lost (16:7–11). He will teach you the Word (14:26) and use it in your life to glorify Christ (16:12–15).*

What Judas knew (21–30). Jesus did not reveal Judas's secret; in fact, He treated him just like the others and they detected nothing amiss. What love that Jesus should not only protect the man who betrayed Him but even wash his feet! Jesus with the towel is the perfect example of humility; Judas with the bread is a perfect example of hypocrisy and treachery.

What the world must know (31–38). The distinguishing mark of true disciples is their love for one another (1 John 2:7-11), and it is the kind of love that the world can see. He commands us to love, and He gives us the power to obey (Rom. 5:5).

JOHN 14

No wonder the disciples were troubled (vv. 1, 27): Jesus was going to leave them, one of them would betray Him, and Peter would deny Him. Jesus encouraged them by telling them about Himself and the Father.

Jesus takes us to the Father (1–6). We have a home in heaven when life is over, and we shall meet Jesus and the Father. James M. Gray wrote, "Who could mind the journey when the road leads home?" Blessed assurance!

Jesus reveals the Father (7–11). In what He said (7:16) and did (5:19) during His earthly ministry, Jesus revealed the Father: "I and My Father are one" (10:30). How can we not love the Father when He is like Jesus?

Jesus glorifies the Father (12–18). He does it through His people as they do God's works and keep His commandments. Apart from the power of the Holy Spirit and prayer, we could never glorify the Lord.

Jesus and the Father dwell with us (19–31). It is one thing for us to go to heaven and quite something else for heaven to come to us! There is a deeper fellowship with the Son and the Father for those who love Him, seek Him, and obey Him. We experience His peace as we commune with the Father and the Son in love.

Jesus is the way to the Father; He reveals the truth about the Father; and He shares the life of the Father with us. Why should our hearts be troubled?

JOHN 15

His life (1–8). A branch is good for only one thing—bearing fruit. It may be weak in itself, but it has a living relationship with the vine and can be productive. To abide in Christ means to be in communion with Him so that our lives please Him. We know that we are abiding when the Father prunes us, cutting away the good so that we can produce the best. We glorify God with fruit, more fruit, much fruit.

His love (9–17). Abiding depends on obeying, and obeying depends on loving. Love and joy go together and make it easy for us to obey His will. We should love Him, love His will, and love one another. Note the "fruit of the Spirit": love (v. 10), joy (v. 11), and peace (14:27; Gal. 5:22).

His name (18–27). We enjoy the love of Christ and of the brethren, but we also must endure the hatred of the world for His name's sake. The more we are like Christ, the more the world system will oppose us. Depend on the Spirit's power and you will be a fruitful, faithful Christian (vv. 26–27).

JOHN 16

The world's opposition (1–15). The Lord warned them about the opposition that would come. Do not be surprised when you are persecuted by religious people (v. 2), for this has been going on ever since Cain killed Abel (Gen. 4; Luke 11:47–51). The Spirit helps us witness to the world and glorify Christ before the world (Acts 4:8ff.), so depend on Him.

The world's joy (16–24). When Jesus was arrested, crucified, and buried, the world system rejoiced because their Enemy was out of the way. But today He is alive, and we have every reason to rejoice! The Lord does not *replace* our sorrow with joy; He *transforms* our sorrow into joy. The same baby that gives the mother pain also gives her joy. The world's joy does not last, but the believer's joy is forever (Ps. 16:11).

The world's defeat (25–33). In the next few hours, the disciples would watch their world fall apart; and yet Jesus assured them that He was the winner. "I have overcome the world" is a fact, not a promise, and it applies to us today. We are overcomers through Him (1 John 5:1–5).

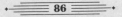

JOHN 17

In this, his high priestly prayer, Jesus prayed for Himself (vv. 1–5), His disciples (vv. 6–19), and all of His church (vv. 20–26).

The prayer reveals our Lord's spiritual priorities: glorifying the Father (v. 1), the unity of the church (vv. 21–23), the sanctity of the church (v. 17), and the winning of a lost world (vv. 18–19). Are these priorities in your life?

It also reveals the gifts He has given His people: eternal life (vv. 2–3), the Word (vv. 8, 14), and His glory (v. 22). But note that believers are the Father's gift to Him (vv. 2, 6, 9, 11–12), just as Jesus is the Father's love gift to us (3:16). It is all of grace!

The word *world* appears nineteen times in this prayer, for this prayer tells us how to "overcome the world" (16:33). We must seek God's glory first (vv. 1–5), experience His joy (v. 13), be sanctified by the Word (v. 17), seek to win the lost (vv. 18–19), and encourage the unity of God's people (vv. 20–23).

Judas the Lost	*Judas was not a saved man, even though he was one of the Twelve. He never believed in Jesus (6:66–71) and therefore was never washed from his sins (13:11). He was not chosen by Christ (13:18) and therefore not kept (17:12). Judas is a frightening example of how near one can get to the kingdom and still be lost.*

Glory is another key word. Christ laid aside His glory to come to earth (v. 5b), glorified God on earth (v. 4), and was glorified when He returned to heaven (v. 5a). Christ is glorified in His church (v. 10) and has shared His glory with the church (vv. 22, 24). We already have the glory; we are just waiting for it to be fully revealed (Rom. 8:18–21, 30).

The Scottish Reformer John Knox had this prayer read to him daily during his last illness. But you would benefit by starting now to read it and meditate on it. What a treasury of truth it is!

JOHN 18

Judas depended on the strength of numbers, Peter on the strength of his arm, Annas and Caiaphas on the strength of their position, but Jesus on the strength of love and devotion to the Father. Jesus had a cup in His hand, not a sword, but that cup was His scepter. He was in complete control.

On the other hand, Peter fought when he should have yielded and followed when he should have fled. Yielding and fleeing looked like defeat, but they were the Father's will; and Peter should have obeyed. While Jesus was giving His witness to the high priest, Peter was denying the Lord. Which was the successful witness, Peter or Jesus?

As a Roman governor, Pilate was worried about the threat of another kingdom. Verse 36 is certainly a rebuke to believers who follow the example of Peter. At Pentecost, Peter wielded the sword of the Spirit and won a victory.

JOHN 19

The crown (1–16). Jesus and Pilate had been talking about a kingdom, so it was only right that the King have a crown. It was meant for mockery, but it preached a message, for Jesus was wearing the consequences of Adam's sins (Gen. 3:17–19). But a crown is a sign of victory. He has overcome!

The cross (17–27). Jesus started out bearing His own cross, but then Simon was drafted to carry it for Him (Mark 15:21). We are not told why, although tradition says that Jesus fell and could not carry it. Considering all He had been through, that is not difficult to believe. Criminals carried the cross as a sign of guilt, *and Jesus was not guilty!*

The conquest (28–42). "It is finished!" was the cry of a conqueror. Jesus accomplished what all of the old covenant sacrifices could not do (Heb. 10:1–18). The prophecies and types were fulfilled and the sacrifice for sins made once and for all forever. It was not a martyr that Joseph and Nicodemus put into the tomb; it was a victor.

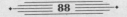

> **Our Final Payment**
>
> The Greek word translated "It is finished!" was a familiar word in that day. Bankers used it when the final payment had been made on a debt. Jesus completely paid the debt we owed, and it will be remembered against us no more forever. Hallelujah, what a Savior!

JOHN 20

Confusion (1–10). Mary jumped to conclusions and soon had Peter and John on the run. They were busy, but they had nothing to say and were accomplishing little. They saw the evidence for the Resurrection, but it did not change their lives. They needed a meeting with the living Christ.

Love (11–18). Unbelief blinds our eyes to the Lord's presence. When He speaks His word to us, faith and love are rekindled. Mary was changed from a mourner to a missionary when she met the living Lord.

Peace (19–23). Locked doors will not give you peace, nor will they keep out your loving Savior. He comes with the message of peace based on His sacrifice on the cross (v. 20; Rom. 5:1).

Faith (24–31). The Lord tenderly deals with our doubts and unbelief. We today cannot see Him or feel His wounds, but we have the Word of God to assure us (vv. 9, 30–31). When your faith falters, do not ask for signs. Open His Word and let Him reassure you.

JOHN 21

Jesus the Stranger (1–4). When Peter returned to the old life, he took six other men with him. Their work was in vain (15:5) because the Lord was not with them. How kind He is to come to us when we have disobeyed Him and have failed in our work!

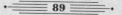

Jesus the Master (5–8). When Jesus takes charge, failure is turned into success; and the difference was only the width of the ship! You never know how close you are to victory, so admit your failure and obey what He tells you to do. He never fails.

Jesus the Host (9–14). It took six men to drag the net (v. 8), but Peter did it alone when Jesus gave the orders (v. 11). We should always remember that "God's commandment is God's enablement." Did the fire of coals remind Peter of his denials (18:18ff.)? Did the miraculous catch of fish remind him of his call to service (Luke 5:1–11)? How kind of Jesus to feed Peter before dealing with him about his sins!

Jesus the Shepherd (15–17). The most important thing in ministry is loving Christ, for all ministry flows from that. Peter the fisherman was also to be a shepherd and care for the lambs and sheep.

Jesus the Lord (18–25). By saying, "Follow Me," Jesus reinstated Peter as an apostle. But Peter turned around and took his eyes off the Lord (Matt. 14:30), and Jesus had to rebuke him. The next time you are tempted to meddle in somebody else's ministry, ponder Christ's words: "What is that to you? You follow Me!" (v. 22).

Peter followed the Lord right into the excitement of the book of Acts!

ACTS

$\blacklozenge$

Perhaps a better title is "The Acts of the Holy Spirit through the Church." This story tells how God's people obeyed the Lord's commission to take the gospel to the whole world. Luke wrote it as a companion volume to his gospel (1:1–3; Luke 1:1–4), and it describes what Jesus *continued to do and teach* after He returned to heaven.

Peter's ministry dominates the first part of the book (chaps. 1—12), and then Luke focuses on Paul's ministry (chaps. 13—28). These two men had parallel experiences of both trial and ministry. Peter used the "keys" (Matt. 16:19) to open the door of faith to the Jews (chap. 2), the Samaritans (chap. 8), and the Gentiles (chap. 10); Paul took the good news to the Gentiles in the Roman Empire.

Acts 1:8 outlines the book, for the gospel went from Jerusalem (chaps. 1—7) to Judea and Samaria (chaps. 8—9) and then to the ends of the earth (chaps. 10—28). The book of Acts describes a transition from ministry to Jews to ministry to the Gentiles and explains how the gospel got from Jerusalem to Rome.

This book is for every Christian who wants to experience the power of the Holy Spirit and be a witness for Jesus Christ "to the end of the earth" (1:8). Ask God what part He wants you to play in taking the gospel to the whole world, starting right where you are. "Lord, what do You want me to do?" (9:6).

ACTS 1

One hundred and twenty ordinary people hardly constitute an imposing army; but in a few days, they would make an impact that is being felt even today. The same resources God gave them are still available to us.

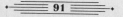

A living Lord (1–3). Christ is the Head of the church (Eph. 1:22; 4:15) and supplies life to His body, giving dynamic and direction to His people. What He began to do and teach, the church continues as He guides and empowers through His Spirit.

The power of the Spirit (4–8). God's power is available to God's people who want to do His will and be His witnesses. You do not have to be an apostle to have the power of the Spirit in your life (Eph. 5:18).

The promise of His return (9–11). He is the Lord of history, working out His purposes in this world. The church may lose some battles, but we will win the war!

Trust God's Guidance

If we are faithful to read God's Word, study it, meditate on it, and obey it, God will guide us when we have decisions to make. The Holy Spirit teaches us (John 14:26; 16:13–14) and directs us when we pray and seek the Lord's will. The Holy Spirit uses truth, not ignorance; so the more facts we have, the better. We should use our common sense but not lean on it (Prov. 3:5–6), for we walk by faith and not by sight. If we sincerely move in the wrong direction, the Lord will show us (Acts 16:6–10; Phil. 3:15), so we need not fear. It is good for believers to read the Word and pray together as they seek the mind of the Lord.

The power of prayer (12–14, 24–26). God shares His power with us as we pray and ask Him for His help. Throughout Acts, notice Luke's emphasis on prayer. The first church was a praying church.

The guidance of Scripture (15–23). His Word is still our lamp and light (Ps. 119:105), and we must obey what it says. God guides His people when they are willing to follow.

ACTS 2

The Spirit came, not because the believers prayed but because the day of Pentecost had come, the day appointed for the "birthday of the church" (Lev. 23:15–21). He baptized the believers into one body (1 Cor. 12:13) so that they had a living connection with their Head exalted in heaven. Luke 2 describes the birth of the Lord's *physical* body and Acts 2 the birth of His *spiritual* body.

The Spirit also filled the believers and empowered them for witness. He gave Peter insight into the Word and the ability to show men Christ in the Word. The Spirit used the witness of the church to convict the lost, just as Jesus said He would do (16:7–10).

The Gift of Tongues

The believers praised God in "other tongues," that is, known languages understood by the people present (Acts 2:6–11). The apostles worshiped and praised God in tongues (v. 11) but preached the gospel in Aramaic, a tongue the Jews could understand. During the transition in ministry from Jews to Gentiles, each time Peter used the "keys," the gift of tongues was evident: among the Jews (2:1–4), the Samaritans (8:14ff.), and the Gentiles (10:44–48). Not all believers speak in tongues (1 Cor. 12:30), and it is not identified as one of the most important gifts (1 Cor. 12:7–11).

But the same Holy Spirit assisted the believers in their church fellowship (vv. 40–47). The original group was outnumbered by the new believers, but there was still harmony in the church family. They worshiped daily and witnessed daily, and "the Lord added to the church daily" (v. 47). Is your experience with the Lord a *daily* one?

ACTS 3

Priorities. Peter and John were not so caught up with large crowds that they had no time for individuals. Nor were they so busy in ministry that they could not pray. They had learned their lessons well from the Lord Jesus (Mark 1:35; Luke 8:40ff.).

Power. The emphasis in chapters 3–4 is on the name of Jesus (3:6, 13, 16, 20, 26; 4:2, 7, 10, 12, 17–18), the name above every name (Phil. 2:9–11). Faith in the name of Jesus releases power so that lives are changed. To pray or minister in His name means to ask or act on His authority (Matt. 28:18–20) so that He alone gets the glory.

Proclamation. At Pentecost, the sound of a rushing wind drew the crowd (2:2, 6); but here the witness of a changed life brought the people together. Thus, Peter had the opportunity to preach, and two thousand people were converted. Reach out to the individual (v. 7) and God will give you opportunities for a bigger harvest (John 4:28ff.).

❝*It's the individual touch that tells. He [Jesus] doesn't love in the mass, but in ones.*❞

Amy Carmichael

ACTS 4

In his sermon at Pentecost, Peter proved from the Scriptures that Jesus was alive; but now he proved it by the miraculous change in the beggar's life. The man was healed through the power of the name of Jesus. The Sadducees did not believe in resurrection (23:6–8), so they wanted to put a stop to the ministry of the apostles. This was the beginning of the official persecution of Christians.

What do you do when they tell you to stop sharing the gospel? What did the apostles do? Certainly they recalled the words of Jesus Christ (Matt. 10:16–26) and depended on the Holy Spirit to help them. Furthermore, they were so filled with their message and with love for Christ that they could not stop telling people about Him!

They depended on prayer (vv. 23–31) and directed their prayer to a sovereign God who made everything and can do anything. They based their petitions on Psalm 2, a marvelous psalm to read when you are being attacked.

When you are "let go," where do you go (v. 23)? When you are in trouble, to whom do you turn?

ACTS 5

Pretending (1–11). Barnabas's gift (4:36–37) exposed the sin of Ananias and Sapphira, just as Mary's gift exposed Judas's sin (John 12). The couple lied to the Spirit, to the church, and to Peter; and it cost them their lives. Their sin was not in taking money from God but in pretending to be something they were not.

Obeying (12–16). Dealing with sin in the church often results in new power for the church. Can you imagine a church so spiritual that people were afraid to join with them? Even Peter's shadow had power!

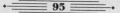

> **❝**We make our decisions, and then our decisions turn around and make us.**❞**
>
> F. W. Boreham

Opposing (17–32). Because the Sadducees could not tolerate evidences of resurrection power, they arrested the apostles again and told them to be quiet. "We ought to obey God rather than men" (v. 29) is the only position to hold when you have the Word of God on your side. Be sure it is conviction and not just opinion.

Hesitating (33–42). Gamaliel advised neutrality, which means avoiding the truth and letting Satan move in (Matt. 12:30, 43–45). With all the evidence they had seen, the council's neutrality was actually dishonesty. If you followed Gamaliel's advice in any area of life—science, cooking, finance—it would lead to paralysis and then death.

❝There is no more miserable human being than one in whom nothing is habitual but indecision.**❞**

William James

ACTS 6

When you yield yourself to do God's will, you never know what challenges you will face.

Serving tables (1–7). No ministry is unimportant for a Christlike servant, for Jesus said, "I am among you as the One who serves" (Luke 22:27). In serving tables, the men released the apostles for their ministry of prayer and the Word; and the result was an increase in conversions (v. 7). People filled with the Spirit see no small jobs or big places. They see only their Master and the opportunity to glorify Him.

Doing wonders (8). From serving tables to doing miracles! Stephen reached out to the lost and sought to win them to Christ. If you are faithful with a few things, the Lord may give you many things (Matt. 25:21).

Facing enemies (9–15). The unbelievers treated Stephen the way the Sanhedrin treated Jesus: they arrested him on trumped-up charges and hired false witnesses to testify. Stephen experienced "the fellowship of His sufferings" (Phil. 3:10), and so will you if your witness hits home (Matt. 5:11–12). They said Stephen was opposing Moses, but he had a shining face just like Moses (Exod. 34)!

Tradition or Truth?

They accused Stephen of being unorthodox in his beliefs (Acts 6:13); but yesterday's orthodoxy had become today's heresy, and the council was behind the times! The Law had been nailed to the cross (Col. 2:14), and the veil of the temple had been torn in two. Within a few years, both the city and the temple would be gone, and Hosea 3:4 would be fulfilled. Are you following man's tradition or God's truth?

> **"**There are many of us that are willing to do great things for the Lord; but few of us are willing to do little things.**"**
>
> D. L. Moody

ACTS 7

The main thrust of Stephen's message is that Israel always resisted the truth and rejected the deliverers God sent to them. They opposed Moses and repeatedly wanted to return to Egypt. They opposed Joseph, and he later became their redeemer! They rejected the many prophets God sent to warn them and call them back to His way. Finally, they rejected their own Messiah and crucified Him.

Israel's history reveals the patience of God and the hardness of man's heart. But it also reveals a ray of hope: Israel rejected their deliverers the first time *but accepted them the second time.* That was true of Moses and Joseph, and it will be true of Jesus when He returns (Zech. 12:10).

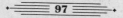

Stephen's death was the third murder in Israel's history and a turning point in God's dealings with the nation. They had rejected the Father when they allowed John the Baptist to be slain; they had rejected the Son when they asked for Jesus to be crucified; and now they had rejected the Holy Spirit. There could be no more forgiveness (Matt. 12:31–32). The line had been crossed, and the gospel moved out to Judea and Samaria.

Stephen

The name Stephen means "a crown," and he won the crown of life because he was faithful unto death (Rev. 2:10).

ACTS 8

The death of Stephen seemed to be a defeat for the church, but it resulted in some great victories for the Lord. Wherever the believers went, they shared the gospel and many trusted the Savior (vv. 1–7; 11:19). Stephen's witness made a tremendous impression on Saul and was instrumental in his conversion (22:20). Never give up when the enemy seems to be winning. It may be your finest hour of victory.

❝*I live for souls and for eternity, I want to win some soul to Christ. If you want this and work for it, eternity alone can tell the result.***❞**

D. L. Moody

Like Stephen, Philip was a deacon who was also an evangelist; and God led him to witness in Samaria to people hostile to the Jews (John 4:9). The coming of Peter and John and the giving of the Holy Spirit linked the Samaritan believers to the saints in Jerusalem and the ancient division was healed. The way to turn enemies into friends is to make them brothers and sisters in Christ.

In times of great blessing, wherever God sows true seed, the devil sows a counterfeit (Matt. 13:24–30, 36–43). Like Peter, we must be alert and exercise discernment.

Philip left a great harvest to talk to one man, but that is the mark of a true servant of the Lord. We must go where God sends us, do what God tells us, and leave the results with Him.

ACTS 9

The conversion of Saul of Tarsus was a turning point in the church's history, and God used several people to touch his life. We remember Paul and are prone to forget the people who helped him get started.

The witness of Stephen was significant (22:20) as were the testimonies and prayers of persons Saul persecuted (Matt. 5:44). Ananias baptized him and encouraged him, and the disciples at Damascus saved his life. When the church in Jerusalem feared to welcome Saul into their fellowship, Barnabas ("son of encouragement") built the bridge. Barnabas later enlisted Saul to serve in the Antioch church (11:25–26) and traveled with him in evangelistic ministry among the Gentiles (13:1–3).

You may not be called to a prominent work as Saul was, but you can do the job God has called you to do and be an encouragement to others. We do not know the names of the brave men who smuggled Saul out of Damascus (v. 25), but holding the ropes was an important job!

ACTS 10

Peter uses the "keys" for the third and last time as he opens the door of faith to the Gentiles. How wonderful is the providence of God! Paul, the apostle to the Gentiles, was being prepared for his life's work; and Peter was about to break down the ancient barriers between Jews and Gentiles: "Known to God from eternity are all His works" (15:18).

But God had to prepare both Peter and Cornelius. He

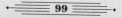

spoke to Cornelius while he was praying and to Peter while he was relaxing. Be alert to the voice of God; you never know when He may have a word for you.

"Not so, Lord! For I have never . . ." (v. 14) is the response that leads to defeat. God was about to do a new thing, and Peter wanted to hold on to the old. He calls Him Lord but refuses to obey Him! Yet God tenderly instructed Peter, and the apostle surrendered to His will.

Peter did not get to finish his sermon. When he said, "Whosoever believes in Him will receive remission of sins" (v. 43), they believed and were saved. What a great way to stop a sermon!

❝ *You can say 'Lord,' and you can say 'Not so,'*
but you cannot say, 'Not so, Lord.' **❞**

W. Graham Scroggie

ACTS 11

Some people make things happen. Peter was available to the Lord, and God used him to officially bring gentile believers into the church. The wall between Jews and Gentiles had been broken down (Eph. 2:11ff.)! The news was astounding to the Jewish believers, for they thought the Gentiles must first become Jewish proselytes before they could become Christians. Thank God that Peter was the kind of person who makes things happen!

Some people hear that things happen. This category may include most of us, but how do you respond when you hear that God has done something new? Do you sincerely try to get the facts, or do you depend on hearsay? We are to "test all things; hold fast what is good" (1 Thess. 5:22).

Some people oppose things happening. The legalistic members of the Jerusalem assembly attacked Peter for eating with the Gentiles, so he explained how God had led. He proved from Scripture (v. 16; 1:5) that what happened was the will of God, and his explanation silenced his critics for the time. How-

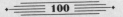

ever, the legalistic element in the church would rise again (chap. 15) and seek to limit the freedom of the gospel.

Some people help other people make things happen. Barnabas enlisted Saul (vv. 25-26) and put him to work in the Antioch church, which led to their going together to the Gentiles with the message of salvation. Barnabas lived up to his name of "son of encouragement."

He Worked for the Great Physician

John Calvin's physician told him to stop working or he would die, and Calvin replied, "Would you have my Master come and find me loitering?"

ACTS 12

The will of the Lord is always wise and good, but it is not always predictable. God spared Peter but allowed James to be killed. He did not deliver Peter from prison until the last minute. He allowed Herod to slay James, but He did not permit the king to act like a god. Is that how *you* would have done it?

Some Christians are like Job's friends: they think they always know exactly what God is doing, will do, and wants done; but they may be wrong. Whenever you are tempted to "play God" in somebody's life, ponder Isaiah 55:8-9.

It is always right to pray, even if your faith is so weak you are surprised when the answer comes! Keep knocking—God opens doors.

ACTS 13

Opportunities come to people busy serving the Lord. God calls people who take time to worship and minister to the Lord. If you want God's guidance, get busy where you are, and He will show you the next step.

Opportunities usually produce opposition (1 Cor. 16:9).

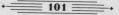

Here is another example of the parable of the tares (Matt. 13:24–30, 36–43): God sowed the good seed (Paul and Barnabas), and Satan sowed a counterfeit.

Opportunities reveal character. Paul and Barnabas kept going, but John Mark returned home. We do not know why, nor should we pass judgment (1 Cor. 10:12). Barnabas reclaimed John Mark (15:36–41) and Paul eventually accepted him (2 Tim. 4:11).

Opportunities develop leadership. The trip began with "Barnabas and Saul" (v. 2), but it became "Paul and his party" (v. 13). Barnabas rejoiced to see Paul being used so mightily of God (Rom. 12:9–11). It was a team effort, and the vital thing was the glory of God.

His Word Endures Forever	*Note the emphasis in Acts 13 on the Word of God (vv. 5, 7, 15, 26, 44, 46, 48–49). In his preaching, Paul quoted from 1 Samuel, Isaiah, Habakkuk, and Psalms. He preached salvation by faith in Jesus Christ whom God raised from the dead (vv. 38–39). Our words do not last, but the Word of the Lord endures forever.*

ACTS 14

Paul was a man on the move but not a man easily moved because of difficulties. "But none of these things move me" was his testimony of faith (20:24), and he lived it.

When he and Barnabas were expelled from Antioch in Pisidia, they shook off the dust of their feet and went to Iconium (13:50–52; Luke 10:11). When the people there tried to stone them, they went to Lystra where they were treated like gods! (That was a greater danger than persecution.) Crowds are fickle: they changed their minds and stoned Paul, but he just got up and went to Derbe.

That was not all. Paul and Barnabas had the courage to retrace their steps so they could help and encourage the new Christians! And when they returned home, they told the church what the Lord had done, not what they had suffered.

Paul and Barnabas put Christ first, others second, and themselves last. They had a job to do, and they were determined by God's grace to do it. How much does it take to move you out of the will of God?

> **"**The will to persevere is often the difference between failure and success.**"**
>
> David Sarnoff

ACTS 15

When God opens a door (14:27), the enemy has somebody handy to try to close it. In this case, the legalists from Judea visited the Antioch church and taught that Gentiles must become Jews before they can be Christians. Their teaching was a denial of salvation by grace through faith (10:43; Eph. 2:8–9).

It was difficult for the orthodox Jews to see that their glorious religious system, given by God, had been fulfilled in Christ and was now out-of-date. (That is why the book of Hebrews was written.) Rather than abandon it, they tried to blend the old religion with the new (Matt. 9:14–17).

When sincere Christians disagree, they must get together, see what God is doing in His church, and find out what the Word has to say about it. Peter, Paul, and Barnabas told what God was doing among the Gentiles, and James related it to the Word (Amos 9:11–12).

In the decision, there was no compromise doctrinally, but there was consideration practically. In the decree, the church asked the Gentiles not to deliberately offend the Jews. You will find the expansion of this principle, the basic principle of love, in Romans 14—15 and 1 Corinthians 8—10.

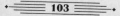

ACTS 16

Paul wrote, "But in all things we commend ourselves as ministers of God: in much patience" (2 Cor. 6:4). See the patience of Paul . . .

In waiting for a helper (1–5). Timothy replaced John Mark and became a true son in the faith to Paul. God has the right person ready at the right time, so be patient.

In seeking God's will (6–10). He was an apostle, yet he did not always know the direction God wanted him to take. He took steps, God closed doors, so he waited; and then God showed him the way.

In ministering the Word (11–15). They waited "some days" before seeking a place to witness, and God had hearts all prepared.

In bearing annoyance (16–18). Paul put up with the demonic promotion as long as he could and then cast out the demon. Paul knew that his action would create problems for him, and it did.

In enduring suffering (19–25). Paul did not use his Roman citizenship to protect himself from pain (22:22–29), but later he used it to protect the new church (vv. 35–40). When you hurt, ask God to give you songs in the night (Ps. 42:8).

In winning a lost soul (26–34). Paul had his eyes on the keeper of the prison and in kindness won him to Christ. How much are we willing to suffer to win someone to the Lord, especially someone who has hurt us?

❝Patience is power. With time and patience,
the mulberry leaf becomes silk.**❞**

Chinese Proverb

ACTS 17

Rejecting the new (1–9). The Jews in Thessalonica were not interested in the new faith or the "new king" that Paul preached, but the Gentile "God seekers" accepted the gospel and were saved. Read 1 Thessalonians 1 to see the change they experienced.

Investigating the new (10–15). The next town was just the opposite! The Jews in Berea took time to examine the evidence and study the Scriptures. There are fair-minded people in every nation, and God knows who they are.

Looking for the new (16–34). The people in Athens "spent their time in nothing else but either to tell or to hear some new thing" (v. 21). How like our world today! The quest for novelty overshadows the search for reality. Paul's sermon was a masterpiece of tact and teaching, and a few people were converted. Paul offered them "newness of life" through the Resurrection (Rom. 6:4), and most of the listeners rejected it.

ACTS 18

The tentmaker (1–3). All Jewish rabbis had a trade because they did not charge their pupils for their lessons. Paul worked hard to support himself and his associates in their ministry. He also worked so that the unsaved could not accuse him of preaching the gospel just to make money (1 Cor. 9). What sacrifices do we make today to further the gospel?

The watchman (4–6). The image is from Ezekiel 3:16–21. As a faithful watchman, Paul warned sinners of the wrath to come, so his hands were free from their blood.

He Is with Us

"I am with you" is a promise God gave to Isaac (Gen. 26:24), Jacob (Gen. 28:15), the Jewish remnant returning from Babylon (Isa. 41:10; 43:5), Jeremiah (Jer. 1:8, 19; 15:20), and the Jews rebuilding the temple (Hag. 1:13; 2:4); and Jesus gave it to us (Matt. 28:20). He said, "I will never leave you nor forsake you" (Heb. 13:5).

The evangelist (7–10). Paul moved next door to the synagogue and kept witnessing! He was not one to run away from either the battlefield or the harvestfield. The Lord promised, "I am with you" (v. 10), a promise He gave to many people and still gives to us today (Isa. 41:10; Matt. 28:20).

A Godly Couple	Aquila and Priscilla, husband and wife, appear several times in apostolic history and were important workers in the early church. They are always mentioned together because they were a team. Being Jews, they were expelled from Rome; as a result, they met Paul in Corinth and opened their home to him. Paul left them in Ephesus where they helped Apollos better understand the gospel (Acts 18:18–28). They returned to Rome where they had a church in their home (Rom. 16:3–5). We do not know how they risked their lives for Paul; but their actions show how much they loved him. They were with Paul in Ephesus when he wrote 1 Corinthians (1 Cor. 16:8, 19), so perhaps it had something to do with the riot described in Acts 19. In his last epistle, Paul sent loving greetings to them (2 Tim. 4:19). Every pastor is grateful to God for couples like Priscilla and Aquila whose hearts, hands, and homes are completely given to the Lord.

The builder (11–28). Paul did not just win souls; he also built a local church by teaching the converts the Word of God

(1 Cor. 3:9–23). In fact, he followed the commission of Matthew 28:18–20. After reporting to his home base in Antioch, Paul revisited some churches to build them up in the faith.

ACTS 19

We read in this chapter that "the word of the Lord grew mightily and prevailed" (v. 20). When does this happen?

When we confirm our faith (1–10). When you believe in Jesus Christ, you receive the gift of the Holy Spirit (Acts 10:43–48; Rom. 8:9). Many people think they are converted but do not have the Spirit's witness within (1 John 5:9–13). Paul could not build a church on men with an inadequate spiritual experience, nor can we today. We must be honest with God.

When we confess our sins (11–20). The devil is a great imitator, but in this case, his attempt was a humiliating failure. The Lord used it for good, because the believers became convicted about their secret sins and confessed them. Then the Spirit could work in mighty power, and the Word increased!

When we confront the enemy (21–41). Paul did not openly attack their idolatry by picketing the temple of Diana or petitioning the city government. He simply shared the Word, and lives were changed. Of course, the real issue was money, not religion. Paul was wise not to go into the theater, although we admire him for his courage. But the riot only called attention to the gospel and gave the believers more opportunity to witness.

Circumstances that look like obstacles are really opportunities when you let God work.

ACTS 20

The uproars usually cease, so be patient; but be sure to get ready for the next battle.

Paul was going to Jerusalem. Along the way, he met with dear friends, ministered the Word, and even enjoyed a quiet voyage and a refreshing walk (v. 13). God's servants need to get away from people and have time alone to think, meditate, and pray. Paul knew he was facing danger in Jerusalem (vv. 22–23), and he wanted to be prepared spiritually.

In his farewell message to the elders, Paul reviewed his

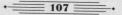

past ministry (vv. 18–21), shared his present concerns (vv. 22–24), and revealed future dangers (vv. 28–31). If you want to catch the heart of Paul, consider his statements: "Serving the Lord . . . I kept back nothing . . . that I may finish my race with joy. . . . It is more blessed to give than to receive."

One day, life will end, and we will have to give our farewell speech. Can we look back without regret and look ahead without fear? Will we finish our race with joy even while others are weeping?

Paul's Roles

As Paul reviewed his ministry in Acts 20:24–26, he saw himself as an accountant ("I count"), a runner ("I may finish my race"), a steward ("the ministry which I received"), a witness ("to testify"), a herald ("preaching the kingdom"), and a watchman ("innocent of the blood"). What a responsibility it is to be a servant of God!

ACTS 21

The traveler (1–14). This farewell journey brought both joy and sorrow to Paul, but life is like that. He knew what lay ahead of him but kept going (Luke 9:51). Years before, the Lord had told him to get out of Jerusalem (22:18). Was he wrong in going back?

The peacemaker (15–25). Paul moved from "the will of the Lord be done" (v. 14) to "do what we tell you" (v. 23). So anxious was Paul to bring unity to the Jews and Gentiles in the church that he agreed to the plan. Was he following "wisdom from above" or "earthly wisdom" (James 3:13–18)? Not every decision we make turns out to bring peace.

The prisoner (26–40). The plan almost worked; on the last day, however, trouble started (v. 27). Of course, their charges

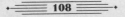

were absurd; yet the mob lives on "suppose" and not fact. Paul had been careful not to cause any unrest in the city (24:10–13), but his efforts had been in vain. He would spend the next five years as a prisoner of Rome.

Sometimes our plans and good intentions seem to bring only trouble. But God is still in control! He used Paul's trials to accomplish His purposes so that His servant got to Rome (23:11). He can do the same for His people today. Walk by faith!

ACTS 22

The *starting point* of Paul's defense was his identification with the Jews (vv. 1–16; 1 Cor. 9:19–23). His birth, training, and early ministry as a rabbi were strictly orthodox. He associated his conversion with Ananias, "a devout man according to the law" (v. 12). He was very tactful, but it takes tact to have contact.

The *turning point* of Paul's defense was his use of the word *Gentiles* (v. 17). Had he not used that word, Paul might have been set free; *but the whole burden of his life was to reach the Gentiles* (Eph. 3:1–13). Paul was arrested because of religious bigotry; his people did not realize that God was doing a new thing in the world.

The *finishing point* was the threat of a scourging, which Paul avoided by asserting his Roman citizenship (vv. 22–29). From then on, it would be one hearing after another and a delay of two years in Caesarea. But God was working out His will in His time, and Paul was willing to wait.

66God is the master of the scenes; we must not choose what part we shall act; it concerns us only to be careful that we do it well, always saying, 'If this please God, let it be as it is.**99**

Jeremy Taylor

ACTS 23

Paul was in danger. If the Romans did not imprison him, the Jews would kill him (22:22). What means did God use to help Paul?

Integrity (1–5). Paul had nothing to hide, and his conscience was clear. Ananias was out of line when he had Paul slapped; but Paul showed respect for the office, not the man.

Strategy (6–10). This did not set Paul free, but it did divide the enemy camp and get the Romans to protect their prisoner better.

Advocacy (11). Paul had the best lawyer available! Christ had assured him when he was in Corinth (18:9–11), and He would assure him again (27:21–25; 2 Tim. 4:16–18). Paul knew that "if God is for us, who can be against us?" (Rom. 8:31).

Opportunity (12–22). Paul's nephew lived in the city, and by the providence of God, he discovered the Jewish plot. Only the Lord could have worked that out. We never know what friend or relative God will use to help us.

Authority (23–35). Paul had the protection of 472 Roman soldiers, and the whole authority of the government was behind him. The Romans did not give Paul a fair hearing, but God still used them to protect Paul and get him to Rome.

ACTS 24

How do the unsaved go about opposing the Lord's servants and their work?

Tertullus started with *flattery* (vv. 2–4), knowing that many people in high places are susceptible to it (12:20–24). Flattery appeals to our pride. If we did not flatter ourselves, others could not successfully flatter us. We really *want* to believe what they say!

Then Tertullus used *slander* (vv. 5–8). Napoleon said, "He who knows how to flatter also knows how to slander." As his last weapon, the lawyer called on *false witnesses* (v. 9) who together supported Tertullus's lies about Paul.

Paul's defense was threefold: his life, his faith and his service to his nation. Although his enemies could not prove their accusations, Paul did not go free. *The safest place for Paul was in that prison,* for God had work for him to do in Rome.

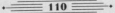

You may not understand why God permits lies to triumph, but leave it all in His hands. He is in control, and the final judgment rests with Him.

> **Don't Delay**
>
> *Actually, Felix was the prisoner, and Paul was the prosecutor. Felix knew he was guilty; but instead of accepting Christ, he delayed. The convenient time to be saved is now (2 Cor. 6:1–2; see also Isa. 55: 6–7).*

ACTS 25

Festus tried to use Paul as a political pawn to win favor with the Jews (vv. 3, 9). If he had succeeded and sent Paul to Jerusalem, the apostle would have been killed. Paul did the wise thing: he used his rights as a Roman citizen and appealed to Caesar. There are times when believers must use the law to protect themselves and the ministry.

But now Festus had a problem. How could he send Paul to Caesar when he had no charges against him that could be proved? God's people sometimes are treated like the guilty even though they are innocent. Remember Joseph, David, Daniel, and Jeremiah, not to mention our Lord Jesus Christ.

In all that happened, God was fulfilling His promise to Paul that he would witness before rulers (9:15) and finally get to Rome (23:11). Being a prisoner and enduring the hearings were difficult for Paul, but he used his opportunities wisely. He believed Jesus' words: "But it will turn out for you as an occasion for testimony" (Luke 21:13).

ACTS 26

Paul saw the light. Instead of defending himself, Paul used the opportunity to present the gospel to King Agrippa and others with him (1 Pet. 3:13–17). When Paul met Jesus on the road to Damascus, he made some important and life-

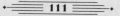

changing discoveries: his religion was out-of-date; his zeal for God was only hurting God; Jesus was alive; and Jesus had a job for Paul to do. Talk about a rude awakening!

The Gentiles need the light. Paul's great learning and zeal would be devoted to the spread of the gospel among the Gentiles (vv. 17-18). Lost sinners are in spiritual darkness and only Christ can give them light.

Agrippa rejected the light. He tried to discredit the message by accusing Paul of being mad, and he tried to minimize his own conviction by his nonchalant reply (v. 28). He turned his back on the light; he was "almost" when he might have been "altogether."

❝Almost persuaded to be a Christian is like the man who was almost pardoned, but he was hanged; like the man who was almost rescued, but he was burned in the house. A man that is almost saved is damned.❞

Charles Spurgeon

ACTS 27

Rejecting Paul's counsel (1-13). What did a Jewish tent-maker know about sailing a ship? So, the advice of the experts (v. 11) and the vote of the majority (v. 12) carried the day. When you are impatient (v. 7) and uncomfortable (v. 12), and when the golden opportunity seems to come along (v. 13), beware! A storm may be brewing!

Hearing Paul's encouragement (14-26). Paul was right to say, "I told you so!" But he followed it with a word of promise from the Lord and a word of encouragement from his believing heart. At a time like that, people needed promises, not preaching.

Following Paul's example (27-38). Paul publicly gave thanks and directed their hearts to God, which encouraged everybody. The weary passengers needed strength for what lay ahead, and that meant taking time to eat. Paul was practical as well as perceptive.

Although Paul started the voyage as a prisoner and passenger, he ended it as the captain of the ship. The ship was lost; but by the grace of God, Paul's presence saved all the passengers. Can the Lord depend on you to sail by faith when you face the storms? Can others depend on you?

ACTS 28

Does anything in this chapter surprise you?

That the natives were kind (1–2, 7–10)? The natives may have been superstitious, but even unsaved people can show concern for those in need. The pagan sailors worked hard to save Jonah before they threw him into the sea (Jon. 1:11–16).

That Paul picked up sticks (3)? If you had saved 276 people from drowning, would you feel it necessary to do menial labor like picking up sticks? Certainly the grateful passengers would have relieved Paul of the task! But Paul was a servant, and he did the job that needed to be done (Phil. 2:1–11).

That Paul was bitten (3–6)? Had he not already been through enough suffering? When Satan cannot win as the lion (1 Pet. 5:8), then he comes as the serpent (2 Cor. 11:3). We must constantly be on guard and trust the Lord to care for us (Mark 16:18).

Paul's Last Years	*Paul was a prisoner in Rome from 61 to 63, and during that time wrote Ephesians, Philippians, Colossians, and Philemon. From 63 to 65, he was free to minister, and he wrote 1 Timothy and Titus. Paul was imprisoned again in 66, wrote 2 Timothy, and was martyred at Rome in late 66 or early 67.*

That Paul welcomed encouragement (11–16)? Even an apostle needs to be encouraged at times, and the saints who met Paul did just that. The group at Appii Forum traveled about ten miles farther than the other group. How far would you go to encourage a fellow believer?

That the Jewish leaders rejected the Word (17–31)? God's chosen people should have known the Scriptures; yet when it was time to decide, the group was divided. But Paul kept witnessing and let God bless the Word as He pleased.

ROMANS

❖

Paul was on his third missionary journey when he wrote the epistle to the Romans, probably from Corinth. He had long planned to visit the believers in Rome, many of whom he knew (chap. 16), and this letter prepared the way. In the letter, he answers the false accusations made about him (3:8; 6:1) and explains why he had not visited Rome sooner (15:23–29). He also gives the grandest presentation of Christian doctrine found anywhere in Scripture.

Romans is one of three books written to explain Habakkuk 2:4: "The just shall live by his faith" (Rom. 1:17; Gal. 3:11; Heb. 10:38). The basic theme is "the just," what it means to be justified (declared righteous by God) and to live a righteous life. *Righteousness* is used in one form or another over forty times.

The book easily falls into three parts: God's righteousness and salvation (chaps. 1–8), God's righteousness and Israel (chaps. 9–11), and God's righteousness and practical Christian living (chaps. 12–16). Romans 1:16–17 is a key statement.

Romans is a closely knit argument that defends the righteousness of God. You can summarize the argument by noting the verses containing "therefore" (3:20, 28; 5:1; 8:1; 12:1).

Justification is God's gracious act by which He *declares* the believing sinner righteous in Jesus Christ because of the work of Christ on the cross. When you believe, Christ's righteousness is *imputed*, that is, "put to your account." Sanctification is God's work in the believer whereby He *imparts* His righteousness and develops holy character and conduct. A righteous standing before God leads to a holy life before men. We are not saved by works or by faith plus works; we are saved by a faith that works (James 2:14–26).

ROMANS 1

The gospel of God (1–17). God has good news! It is *promised* in the Old Testament and centered in Jesus Christ. He came to earth a Jew, died, and arose again; and He saves all who will trust in Him. He alone *purchased* salvation, and this message must be *preached* to the whole world. Why? Because the gospel alone is "the *power* of God to salvation" (v. 16, italics added).

Paul was gripped by the gospel; his whole life was controlled by it. Called to be an apostle (v. 1), he felt himself a debtor to the whole world (v. 14). Through His church, God is calling people to Jesus Christ (vv. 5–7). Has the gospel gripped you?

❝*Religions are man's search for God; the Gospel is God's search for man. There are many religions, but one Gospel.*❞

E. Stanley Jones

Spiritual Debts	God's people are free from the debt of sin, but they are debtors to witness to a lost world (Rom. 1:14), obey the Holy Spirit (8:13), love all people (13:8), encourage their weaker brothers and sisters (15:1), and help the people of Israel (15:25–27). Are you paying your spiritual debts?

The wrath of God (18–32). Paul's main theme is the righteousness of God, but he presents it against the dark background of the judgment of God, *which is going on right now.* Men know God from creation and conscience (vv. 19–20) but refuse to honor Him as God. They live for the creature, not the Creator, and make themselves into gods (v. 25; Gen. 3:4–5). So, God gave them up (vv. 24, 26, 28) and let them suffer the consequences. *The greatest judgment God can inflict on us is to let us have our own way.*

But the same God who delivered up sinners to judgment *delivered up His own Son for lost sinners* (8:32)! That is the gospel. Do you believe it? Are you sharing it?

ROMANS 2

If you know Jesus Christ as your Savior, your sins have already been judged on the cross (John 5:24; Rom. 8:1). But are you ready for the judgment seat of Christ where your works will be judged (Rom. 14:10–12; 2 Cor. 5:10)? Ask yourself the following questions.

Do I judge myself or others (1–3)? How easy it is to cover up my own failures by criticizing others (Matt. 7:1–5)!

Am I grateful for God's goodness (4)? It is not the badness of man but the goodness of God that brings us to repentance (Luke 15:17–19). Do I take God's many blessings for granted?

Is my faith proved by works (5–11)? Paul was not teaching salvation by works but works that prove salvation. Do I obey God's truth and persist in holy living? Do I have a hard heart or a tender heart?

Am I hiding behind religion (12–16, 25–29)? The Jews boasted of their law, but it could not save them. External rituals do not guarantee internal changes. God searches the heart. What does He see in my heart?

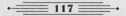

66*How rarely we weigh our neighbor in the same balance in which we weigh ourselves.*99

Thomas a Kempis

Do I practice what I profess (17–24)? Do I tell others what is right but then do what is wrong? Do I expect more of others than I do of myself?

God judges honestly (v. 2) and without partiality (v. 11), and no secret is hidden from Him (v. 16). Are you prepared?

ROMANS 3

Paul, the attorney, summarizes his case.

All are condemned (1-19). Both Jews and Gentiles (religious and irreligious) are guilty before God, and one is no better than the other (v. 9). Paul quotes from Psalms and Isaiah to show that, from head to foot, we are all lost sinners. Do you want to argue about this? Then your mouth has not been stopped! God cannot save you until you say, "Guilty!" and shut your mouth.

We cannot save ourselves (20). The law is a mirror that reveals our sin; only the blood of Christ can wash away our sin. It is good to do good works, but good works are not good enough to save us (Eph. 2:8-9).

God's salvation is lawful (21-31). But how can a *holy* God forgive *guilty* people? Is that lawful? If our judges did that, society would fall apart. But God the Law Giver and Judge obeyed His own law, died for us, and paid the penalty for our sins. The Judge is now the Savior!

Have you shut your mouth, trusted Jesus Christ, and heard God say, "Not guilty"?

ROMANS 4

How was Abraham saved (1-4, 9-12)? Not by works, but by faith (Gen. 15:6). Salvation is not like wages that you earn or works that you can boast about. Abraham was not saved by keeping the law because the law had not been given, nor was he saved by obeying a religious ritual. It was all by God's grace!

How was David saved (5-8)? David wrote Psalm 32 after his great sin with Bathsheba (2 Sam. 11). Can God forgive a man who commits adultery, deceit, and murder? Yes! When David repented and turned to God, he was forgiven, even though the Lord allowed David to feel the bitter consequences of his sins (2 Sam. 12). God justifies *the ungodly,* not the righteous (v. 5; Matt. 9:9-13).

How can you be saved (13-25)? Simply by believing God's

promise as Abraham did. *Faith* and *promise* go together just as *law* and *works* go together. Abraham is the father of the Jewish nation physically, but he is the "father" of all believers spiritually (v. 16; Matt. 3:7-9). At Calvary, our sins were put on Christ's account; when you trust Christ, God puts Christ's righteousness on your account (2 Cor. 5:21). What can be more blessed than to know that your sins are forgiven?

Our Sins Are Covered

Because he preached salvation by grace alone, Paul was accused of promoting sin (Rom. 3:5-8), but the accusation was false. Persons who experience the grace of God in forgiveness have no desire to sin; and if they do sin, they confess it to the Lord (1 John 1:5—2:1). They are tempted (1 Cor. 10:13), and sometimes they fall; but they do not stay down (Ps. 37:23-24). Read all of Psalm 32 to see what God does for His own.

ROMANS 5

In chapter 4, Paul went back to Abraham and David to explain how God declares believing sinners righteous; now he goes all the way back to Adam. Adam's sin passed sin and death on to the whole human race, but Christ's obedience gives righteousness and life to all who trust Him. In our first birth, we became condemned children of Adam; but in our second birth, we are the forgiven children of God. Note the blessings of justification.

Riches (1-5). Peace, access into God's grace, joy, hope, love, the Holy Spirit—what riches we have in Christ! And trials work *for* us, not *against* us, and develop Christian character. How rich we are!

Reconciliation (6-11). We are at peace with God and need

not be afraid. If He did so much for us when we were enemies, think what He will do for us now that we are His children!

Reigning (12–21). When we belonged to the old creation under Adam, death and sin reigned; now that we are in Christ in the new creation (2 Cor. 5:17), grace is reigning, *and we are reigning in life* (v. 17). You can live like a king by the grace of God!

ROMANS 6

Being a Christian is *a matter of life or death* (vv. 1–11). Persons who do not understand the grace of God argue, "If God is gracious, then we should sin more so we receive more grace." Those who trust Christ are identified with Him by the Spirit in His death, burial, and resurrection, as pictured in baptism. The old life is buried! We can reckon it dead (v. 11) and walk in newness of resurrection life.

Being a Christian is *a matter of bondage or freedom* (vv. 12–22). Who is your master, Jesus Christ or the old life? You are not under the authority of Moses (v. 15), but that does not mean you have freedom to break God's moral law (8:1–5). Yield yourself to the Lord; He is the most wonderful Master, and the "salary" He pays lasts forever.

"Alive to God"

The most vivid illustration of Romans 6 is Lazarus (John 11). Jesus raised him from the dead and then said, "Loose him, and let him go" (John 11:44). Lazarus left the grave, got rid of the graveclothes, and began a new life (Col. 3:1ff.). God's people are both "dead" and "alive" (v. 11) and by faith must live accordingly.

Being a Christian is *a matter of rewards or wages* (v. 23). We quote this verse as we witness to the lost, and rightly so; but Paul wrote it originally to believers. Although God forgives the sins of His children, He may not stop the painful consequences of sin. The pleasures of sin are never compensated for by the wages of sin. Sinning is not worth it!

ROMANS 7

Believers are not under the law, but that does not give them license to become outlaws. They have a new life (6:1–11) and a new Master (6:12–23), and they also have a new love: they are *married to Christ* (vv. 1–6). If a marriage must be based on laws instead of love, it is going to make for an unhappy home.

If the law cannot change us or control us, what good is it? Its purpose is to reveal sin, and it does its job well (v. 7). Paul learned that the law even aroused evil desires in him (v. 8). If something as holy as God's law (v. 12) can arouse sinful desires, what wicked sinners we must be!

Law brings out the worst in us, but love brings out the best in us. The Holy Spirit within us helps us to do what God wants us to do (Rom. 8:1–5) and to be what God wants us to be (Gal. 5:22–23). Keep your love relationship with the Lord alive and exciting, and you will have righteousness instead of wretchedness.

A Yielded Life

Romans 7:21–25 does not suggest that you live a divided life because that is impossible. You must choose your Master (6:15–23) and be true to your Husband, Jesus Christ (7:1–6). "The mind" refers to the new nature from God and "the body of death" the old nature from Adam. We cannot serve God with an old nature that is sinful (7:18), but the Holy Spirit enables us to do His will as we yield to Him. The human body is not sinful, but human nature is.

ROMANS 8

Paul asked, "Who will deliver me from this body of death?" (7:24). This chapter gives the answer: the Holy Spirit of God. The blessings He brings make us "more than conquerors" (v. 37)!

Life (1–11). When God saved you, He gave you a new life, not a new law; as you yield to that life, you obey His law. Keep your mind centered on the things of the Lord (Col. 3:1–4) and seek to please God in all things. Let the Spirit live His life in you.

Liberty (12–17). We enter God's family by the new birth, not by adoption (John 3); but adoption gives us an adult standing in His family. He deals with us as mature sons and daughters and not as "little children." We can talk ("Abba, Father" [v. 15]), walk, and use our inheritance right now. We are free, but we are still debtors to the Lord (v. 12).

Hope (18–25). We are not frustrated by the suffering we experience or see in our world because we have hope. When Jesus returns, we will enter into glorious liberty! The Spirit is the beginning of the harvest and assures us that the best is yet to come.

❝*The Holy Spirit longs to reveal to you the deeper things of God. He longs to love through you. He longs to work through you. Through the blessed Holy Spirit you may have: strength for every duty, wisdom for every problem, comfort in every sorrow, joy in His overflowing service.*❞

T. J. Bach

Guidance (26–30). God's purpose is to make His children like His Son, and He will succeed. The Spirit intercedes for us and guides us as we pray, and the circumstances of life work for our good, no matter how painful they may be.

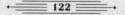

Love (31–39). The Spirit of God makes the love of God real to us (5:5; John 14:23–27). The Father is for us (vv. 31–32), the Son is for us (v. 34), and the Spirit is for us (vv. 26–27). Nothing can separate us from His love. Is there any reason why we should not be "more than conquerors"?

God's People

> In Romans 9—11, Paul's discussion of Israel is not an interruption but an illustration of his theme. He explains Israel's past election (chap. 9), present rejection (chap. 10), and future reception (chap. 11); and he proves that God has been righteous in all His dealings with Israel. God has not failed to work out His divine purposes for the Jews, nor will He fail to work out His purposes for His church.

ROMANS 9

In a part of the Bible that emphasizes the sovereignty of God, We see Paul sorrowing (9:1–3), praying (10:1), and worshiping (11:33–36). He did not feel that God's sovereignty in any way destroyed man's responsibility. The God who ordains the end (saving the lost) also ordains the means to the end, the prayers and witness of His people. They go together.

God is not obligated to save anybody, for all deserve to be condemned. Even Israel was chosen only because of His grace and love (Deut. 7:6–8). Therefore, nobody can criticize God or say He is unfair. That He is merciful to sinners should make us rejoice!

Israel's rejection of Christ did not ruin God's plan, for He went to the Gentiles (Acts 10:1ff.; 15:14) who gladly received the good news. However, God has a remnant among the Jews (vv. 27–29), and believing Jews and Gentiles are one in the church (Eph. 2:11–22).

His mercy endures forever!

God's Part and Our Part

Charles Spurgeon was asked how he reconciled divine sovereignty and human responsibility, and he replied, "I never try to reconcile friends." Augustine said that we must pray as though it all depended on God and work as though it all depended on us. That biblical balance makes for blessing.

ROMANS 10

Why did Israel stumble over Christ and reject Him? Because they did not understand the kind of righteousness God wanted or how to get it. Like the Pharisees (and many people today), they thought only of righteous *works* and could not comprehend a righteousness that comes by faith (v. 13; Joel 2:32; Acts 2:21).

The missionary heart of Paul comes out in verses 14–17. Salvation is by faith, and faith comes "by hearing . . . the word of God" (v. 17). But unbelieving sinners (including Israel) cannot hear unless we tell them. God needs people with beautiful feet (Isa. 52:7) to carry the gospel to the lost.

Despite Paul's broken heart (v. 1) and God's outstretched hands (v. 21; Isa. 65:2), Israel did not believe; but the Gentiles did believe and God saved them! When you feel discouraged in your witnessing, remember Paul; continue caring, praying, and sharing the good news. Keep those feet beautiful!

ROMANS 11

The theology of Romans 9—11 magnifies God's grace and extols His sovereignty. Never lose the wonder of your salvation or of the greatness of God. No matter how deep the valley or difficult the battle, a vision of God's greatness puts joy in your heart and strength in your soul. God knows what He is doing even if you do not understand it fully.

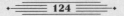

There is a future for Israel; Paul is proof of that (v. 1; 1 Tim. 1:16), and so is Israel's past history (vv. 2–10). God has always had a believing remnant in Israel, no matter how dark the day. When you become discouraged about the future of the church and feel that you may be the only faithful Christian left, read 1 Kings 19 and focus on God's greatness.

We cannot explain all the purposes and plans of God, but we can worship and praise Him for who He is (vv. 33–36). The end result of all Bible study is worship, and the end result of all worship is service to the God we love.

❝Fate says the thing is and must be, so it is decreed. But the true doctrine is—God has appointed this and that, not because it must be, but because it is best that it should be. Fate is blind, but the destiny of Scripture is full of eyes. Fate is stern and adamantine, and has no tears for human sorrow. But the arrangements of providence are kind and good.**❞**

Charles Spurgeon

ROMANS 12

The biblical pattern is to relate doctrine and duty, for what you believe must determine how you behave. In these closing chapters, Paul discusses your relationship with the Lord (12:1–2), yourself (12:3), the church (12:4–16), your enemies (12:17–21), government (chap. 13), and believers who disagree (chaps. 14—15).

Transformation (vv. 1–2). The Spirit of God transforms your life by renewing your mind (2 Cor. 3:18), but He cannot do this unless you give Him your body. When you give yourself to God in spiritual worship, you become a living sacrifice to the glory of God.

Evaluation (3). To think more highly of yourself, *or less highly*, is sin, so have a proper estimate of who you are and what God has given you (Gal. 6:3–5).

Cooperation (4–16). You are part of the body of Christ with a ministry to fulfill, so do your part lovingly and joyfully.

Vindication (17–21). If yours is a godly life, you are bound to have enemies (Matt. 5:10–12; 2 Tim. 3:12); but leave all judgment to the Lord. If you let the Lord have His way, He will use your enemies to build you and make you more like Christ.

ROMANS 13

Believers are citizens of heaven, but we must not minimize our responsibilities on earth. We must be exemplary citizens so that the Lord will be glorified (1 Pet. 2:11–17).

Law (1–7). God has established human government because people are sinners and must be controlled. Governmental authority comes from God, so you must respect the office even if you cannot respect the officer. The fear of punishment is not the highest motivation for obedience, but it is better than having chaos.

Love (8–10). Love for God and for your neighbor is the highest motive for obedience. Love does what is right and just and seeks the best for others. By nature, we do not have this kind of love (Titus 3:3); the Lord gives it to us (Rom. 5:5).

Light (vv. 11–14). Christian citizens live in the light of the Lord's return. Paul admonishes, "Wake up—dress up—clean up—look up!" Are you heeding it?

❝*Whatever makes men good Christians makes them good citizens.*❞

—Daniel Webster

ROMANS 14

Your love may be tested more by Christians who disagree with you than by unbelievers who persecute you. It takes a diamond to cut a diamond. What should you do when your brother or sister disagrees with you about how God's people ought to live?

Acceptance (1–9). Not all believers are mature, and love demands that the mature members of the family defer to the immature. Love protects people and gives them a chance to grow up. People may be difficult, but we must accept them in love for the Lord's sake.

Accountability (10–12). We have no right to judge and condemn one another because the Judge is the Lord. Each believer will have enough to do in keeping his own account right without interfering with others' accounts!

Ambition (13–23). Our desire must not be to get everybody to agree with us; our desire must be to pursue peace, not cause others to stumble, and help others to mature in Christ. What starts as *grieving* (v. 15) can become *offending* (v. 21), *making weak* (v. 21), and *causing others to stumble and fall* (vv. 13, 21). The result might be *destroying* a brother's or sister's faith (vv. 15, 20). Is destroying another just to have your own way worth it?

Gaining Strength	The weak Christian does not yet understand and practice freedom in Jesus Christ. Jewish believers, raised under the law of Moses, had a difficult time adjusting to their new life. Conscience becomes strong as we accept what God says about us in the Word and act on it by faith. However, it takes time for conscience to develop, and we must be patient with one another.

ROMANS 15

A debt to the weak (1–6). The strong must bear the weak and help them grow, and that takes love and patience. If we

live to please ourselves, we will not follow the example of Christ who lived to please the Father and help others.

A debt to the lost (7–21). God saved the Jews so that they might reach the Gentiles and lead them in praising the Lord. God has saved us so that we might win others. We have a debt to pay (1:14).

A debt to Israel (22–33). The Gentiles are indebted to the Jews (John 4:22). And that debt is paid by praying for them (Ps. 122:6), witnessing to them in love, and sharing our material gifts to assist them.

❝To consider persons and events and situations only in the light of their effect upon myself is to live on the doorstep of hell.**❞**

Thomas Merton

ROMANS 16

We are prone to honor Paul and forget the many ordinary people who helped make his ministry possible. Paul was the human author of the epistle to the Romans, but Tertius wrote it down (v. 22), Gaius gave Paul a place to live and work (v. 23), and Phoebe carried the completed letter to Rome. Nobody in God's family is unimportant to Him, and no ministry is insignificant. Find the work He wants you to do and faithfully do it.

There is a "hidden romance of history" that is not recorded in the Bible. When and how did Priscilla and Aquila risk their lives to save Paul (vv. 3–4)? When were Andronicus and Junia in prison with Paul (v. 7)? How was Rufus's mother a mother to Paul (v. 13)? Who were the troublemakers about whom Paul warned the Roman believers (vv. 17–18)? Perhaps one day in heaven we will be given the answers!

Meanwhile, the important thing is that we are obedient to the Lord (v. 19) and lead others into "obedience to the faith"

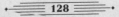

(v. 26). The God of patience and comfort (15:5), the God of hope (15:13), and the God of peace (16:20) will establish you and enable you (16:25).

> *The service we render for others is really the rent we pay for our room on this earth.*
>
> Wilfred Grenfell

FIRST CORINTHIANS

◆

Corinth, the capital of Achaia, was perhaps the richest and most important city in Greece. It was also the most corrupt. A center for trade, Corinth was invaded by all kinds of religions and philosophies. Paul founded the Corinthian church during his second missionary journey (Acts 18) and ministered there a year and a half.

After he left, serious problems developed in the church, and Paul wrote the members a stern letter that was not successful (1 Cor. 5:9). He heard that the church was divided (1:11), and then a delegation from the church arrived in Ephesus with a letter asking Paul's help regarding specific questions. First Corinthians was his response.

Paul dealt with sin in the church (chaps. 1—6), and then he answered the questions they asked (chaps. 7—16; note the repeated phrase, "Now concerning . . ."). He discussed marriage (chap. 7), idolatry (chaps. 8—10), public worship (chap. 11), spiritual gifts (chaps. 12—14), the Resurrection (chap. 15), and the special offering he was taking for the Jews (chap. 16).

Paul had planted a church in the city, but the city had gotten into the church; and that explained why there were so many problems. The believers in Corinth needed to heed Romans 12:2, and so do we today.

1 CORINTHIANS 1

Even though believers are "all one in Christ Jesus" (Gal. 3:28), the local church often suffers from division. Why?

For one thing, we forget the calling we have in Christ (vv. 2, 9, 24—29). It is only by God's grace that we have been called, and this fact should humble us and encourage us to love one another (John 15:17).

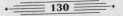

Another factor is our tendency to follow human leaders and develop a fan club mentality. Christ died for us and lives to bless us, and He must have the preeminence.

A third factor is dependence on human wisdom and philosophies, of which there were many in Corinth. The world's wisdom had crept into the church, and it did not mix with the wisdom of God (Isa. 8:20). Various theologies are the attempts of scholars to interpret the Word of God, but they are not the Word. Never allow them to be a cause of division.

1 CORINTHIANS 2

Power (1–5). Paul did not imitate the itinerant teachers in Corinth who depended on their eloquence and intellectual brilliance. Paul's faith was in God, not in himself (Zech. 4:6). He wanted sinners to trust in Christ's power. You may think you lack ability to serve God, but God can turn your weakness into strength. The gospel still works (Rom. 1:16)!

Wisdom (6–16). The Jews asked for demonstrations of power and the Greeks looked for wisdom, both of which are available in Jesus Christ (1:24). A deeper wisdom of God is available for those who are mature (2:12–16). Allow the Spirit of God to teach you about the Son of God from the Word of God, and grow up in Him.

Wisdom and power go together. They need each other, and they keep the Christian life balanced.

1 CORINTHIANS 3

Maturing (1–4). We never outgrow the nourishing milk of the Word (1 Pet. 2:2), but we cannot grow strong unless we also have the "solid food" (Heb. 5:12–14; Matt. 4:4). You grow by eating and exercising (1 Tim. 4:6–8), and it takes both. Age is no guarantee of spiritual maturity.

Harvesting (5–9). Everybody has a place in the Lord's harvest, and all are doing His work (John 4:34–38). There must be no competing or comparing, for the Lord alone recognizes the work and gives the reward. It makes no difference who the servant is so long as Jesus Christ is Lord of the harvest.

Building (10–17). Paul writes about the local church and the materials we put into it as we minister (Prov. 2:1–5; 3:13–

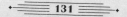

15). Substituting man's wisdom for God's Word means building with perishable materials that will burn up at the judgment seat of Christ.

Glorifying God (18–23). Because the Corinthian believers gloried in human teachers (1:12) and human wisdom, they robbed God of the glory that rightly belonged to Him. "Let no one boast in men" is a command, not a suggestion.

> **❝**If you lack knowledge, go to school. If you lack wisdom, get on your knees! Knowledge is not wisdom. Wisdom is the proper use of knowledge.**❞**
>
> Vance Havner

---

1 CORINTHIANS 4

Life is *a stewardship*, so be faithful (vv. 1–5). We judge ourselves, and others judge us; but the Final Judge is the Lord. Live to please Him alone.

Life is *a gift*, so be humble (vv. 6–9). Your abilities and blessings came from God; you cannot take credit for them. They are God's gift to you, and your use of them is your gift to God. It is sinful to contrast various Christian workers (1:12) because only God knows their hearts.

Life is *a battle*, so be courageous (vv. 9–13). If the apostles were the greatest Christians who ever lived, and they were filth and the scum of the earth, where did that leave the boasting Corinthians?

Life is *a school*, so be teachable (vv. 14–21). Paul saw himself as a father in the Lord who had to instruct and discipline his children. Our Father in heaven uses many hands and voices to teach us, and we must be willing pupils as we go through life.

1 CORINTHIANS 5

Separation (1–7). The background of the chapter is the Passover Feast (Exod. 12). The presence of the immoral man

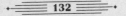

should have turned the feast into a funeral (v. 2), but the church was boasting about the sinner instead of weeping over him. Tolerating known sin in the church is like putting leaven into the Passover Feast: it does not belong.

Celebration (8). Paul saw the Christian life as "keeping the feast" (v. 8), that is, feeding on Christ, being ready to move, and being sure we are not defiled by sin (leaven, yeast). The Lamb has set us free, and we are on our way to our promised inheritance!

Isolation (9–13). Sin in the life of the believer is far worse than sin in the life of an unbeliever. We cannot isolate ourselves from the world, but we can separate ourselves from disobedient believers so that God can discipline them.

Share in Fellowship

The phrase "deliver such a one to Satan" (1 Cor. 5:5) suggests that there is spiritual safety within the fellowship of the local church. To be disciplined and dismissed from fellowship makes us vulnerable to Satan's attacks. Far better to confess our sins, be forgiven, and be restored to fellowship.

---

1 CORINTHIANS 6

Not only were the Corinthian believers compromising with the world, but they were also losing their testimony before the world by taking each other to court before pagan judges. Paul repeatedly asked, "Do you not know?" (vv. 2, 3, 15, 16, 19). They were ignorant of some basic truths of the Christian life.

We will judge angels (1–8). If God entrusts that great a responsibility to His people, can't He help us with our petty decisions today?

We have been changed (9–12). We are not what we once were, so why should we live as we once lived? It is a matter not of "What is lawful?" but of "What is helpful?"

We belong to the Lord (13-20). He made the human body, He dwells in believers by His Spirit, and He purchased us at the Cross. The believer's body belongs to God and must be used to glorify Him.

Flee These Temptations	"Flee sexual immorality" (1 Cor. 6:18) reminds us of Joseph when he fled from Potiphar's wife (Gen. 39). "Flee also youthful lusts" (2 Tim. 2:22) is a parallel admonition. When it comes to the devil, resist him and he will flee from you (James 4:7); but when it comes to temptations of the flesh, you do the fleeing!

1 CORINTHIANS 7

Marriage is *a gift* (vv. 1-9), and not everybody has the same gift. Some people have more self-control than others. People remain unmarried for different reasons (Matt. 19:11-12), and each one must know the will of God.

Marriage is *a ministry* (vv. 10-16). He addressed people who had been converted after marriage and who wondered if they should remain with their unsaved spouses. "Yes," said Paul, "because you might win them to Christ." But even Christian spouses can have a wonderful ministry to each other as they grow in the Lord and love each other (Eph. 5:22ff.).

Marriage is *a calling* (vv. 17-24). When you become a Christian, that does not annul what you were before you trusted Christ. Jews are still Jews, slaves are still slaves, and married people are still married. But now, with the Lord's help, you can fulfill that calling in a greater way.

Marriage is *a challenge* (vv. 25-40). Paul does not deny the blessings of marriage, but he does remind us of the burdens that marriage brings, especially when the times are tough. Building a Christian home is a great ministry, but nobody should enter into it lightly or carelessly.

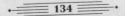

> **"***Success in marriage involves much more than finding the right mate. It also requires being the right mate.***"**

1 CORINTHIANS 8

Life is controlled by conscience. Conscience is the judge within that commends us for doing right and condemns us for doing wrong (Rom. 2:14–15). If we sin against conscience, we do terrible damage to the inner person.

Conscience is strengthened by knowledge. As we grow in spiritual understanding, a weak conscience becomes stronger, and we appreciate our freedom in Christ more and more. The weak believer must not run ahead of his conscience, and the strong believer must never force him to do so.

Knowledge must be balanced by love. Your spiritual knowledge can be either a weapon to hurt people or a tool to build people. If your knowledge puffs you up, it will tear others down. Love knows when and how to yield to others without compromising the truth. Review Romans 14—15.

> **"***Knowledge is proud that he has learned so much;
> Wisdom is humble that he knows no more.***"**
>
> William Cowper

1 CORINTHIANS 9

We do not have the right to give up our freedom, for that was purchased by Christ (Gal. 5:1); *but we do have the freedom to give up our rights.* For the sake of winning the lost (v. 12), Paul gave up his right to receive financial support, and he begged the Corinthians to give up their rights for the sake of the saved.

Christian ministry is like fighting a war, caring for a vineyard, tending a flock, and cultivating a field (vv. 7–11). Meditate on these images, and see what they teach you about serving the Lord.

Ministry is a stewardship (v. 17), and the servant must be faithful (4:2). Ministers of Christ are also like runners who must keep the rules or be disqualified (vv. 24–27).

Verses 19–23 call for courtesy and wisdom in witness, not for compromise. "I have become all things to all men" does not mean Paul had no personal convictions. It means he used his convictions to build bridges, not walls. If he seemed inconsistent, it was only because people did not look deep enough. *His one great desire was to win the lost,* and that governed his every decision.

> **❝**Tact is the art of making a point without making an enemy.**❞**
>
> Howard W. Newton

1 CORINTHIANS 10

If you insist on using your rights, you may cause a weaker believer to stumble; *and you may also bring trouble on yourself.* When you face difficult decisions, take these factors into consideration.

God's blessing (1–5). The parallel to God's people today is obvious. We have been redeemed from the world, identified with Jesus Christ, and nourished by spiritual food and drink. But these blessings are no guarantee that we will be successful.

God's judgment (6–12). When Israel sinned, God disciplined them; and He will do the same to His people today. Do you practice and tolerate in your life any of the sins named here? God gives His children freedom, but the freedom to sin is not included.

God's promise (13–22). God knows how much we can take and always provides the way of escape. Sometimes the smartest thing to do is to flee (v. 14; 6:18). Always look for the open door and the blessing on the other side.

God's glory (23–33). Two extremes must be avoided: practicing license in the name of Christian freedom, and being so fussy that we cannot live in a real world and make rational decisions. When you seek to edify others and glorify the Lord, you will know what to do.

66*When you flee from temptation, be sure you do not leave a forwarding address behind.*99

---

1 CORINTHIANS 11

Some matters discussed in this chapter may have only local significance, but the spiritual principles apply to us today. When it comes to sharing in public worship, we must ask ourselves serious questions.

Do I dishonor authority (1–16)? We must be careful not to dishonor the Lord, no matter what the cultural standards may be. God has established headship in creation and in the church, and we must respect it.

Do I despise the church (17–22)? We are one in Christ and in love must honor one another. By the way they ate their love feast, the rich embarrassed the poor and brought shame to the church.

Do I discern the body (23–34)? When we meet to celebrate the Communion service, we must examine ourselves and not one another; and we must be honest with the Lord as we confess our sins. We discern His body in the bread, but we also discern it in the members of the church who eat with us. The Lord's Supper is a family feast. While it must be personal, it must not become so individual that it becomes selfish. It should be a means of promoting the unity of the church.

1 CORINTHIANS 12

The Corinthian believers were especially gifted by God (1:4–7), but some of them were creating problems by using

their spiritual gifts in unspiritual ways. Paul reminded those people of three basic truths.

There is one Lord (1–11). The Spirit glorifies Christ (John 16:14), not Himself. The Spirit gives us gifts so that we can serve Christ and His church "for the profit of all" (v. 7) and not for our own selfish enjoyment. Have you discovered what the Spirit has given you? Have you thanked God for it, and are you using your gift(s) under Christ's lordship?

There is one body (12–31). As members of the same body, we belong to one another, and we need one another. The believers you think you can do without may be the ones you need the most! We must minister to one another and care for one another as one body.

There is one danger (25). When a part of your physical body declares independence from the other parts, it starts to die and you have to visit the doctor. Division in the local church brings weakness and pain (1:10–17) because no Christian can go it alone and be successful. Do you thank God for fellow Christians and seek to care for them?

> **"**None understand better the nature of real distinction than those who have entered into unity.**"**
>
> Johannes Tauler

1 CORINTHIANS 13

This so-called hymn to love was Paul's prescription for solving the sickness in the church body in Corinth. The believers had spiritual gifts, but they lacked spiritual graces and needed to be reminded why love is so important in the Christian life.

Love puts *quality into service* (vv. 1–3). When you have love, your words and actions amount to something and help other people.

Love also puts *maturity into character* (vv. 4–7). The Corinthians were impatient with each other, suing each other, tolerating sin in the church, and creating problems because they did not have love. Whatever qualities you may have, they are nothing without love.

Love puts *eternity into life* (vv. 8–13). Love lasts, and what love does will last. Love is the greatest and does the greatest because "God is love" (1 John 4:8).

❝*God hates the great things in which love is not the motive power; but He delights in the little things that are prompted by a feeling of love.***❞**

D. L. Moody

---

1 CORINTHIANS 14

Why go to church? God's people assemble for one purpose: to worship God. They worship Him by their praying and singing (v. 15), teaching and preaching (v. 3). Worship should result in glory to God, blessing for God's people (v. 3), and fear and conviction for sinners (vv. 23–25).

But for these things to happen, Jesus Christ must be Lord of our lives, and we must yield to the Holy Spirit. If we come to church to display our spirituality, we will not only miss the blessing ourselves but also cause others to miss the blessing. We come to honor Him.

A key word in this chapter is *edification* (vv. 3–5, 12, 17, 26), which means "building up." A worship service should lift up the Lord and build up the saints, not puff up the participants.

1 CORINTHIANS 15

We have a living Lord (1–19). Jesus is alive, and the gospel message is true! Witnesses who saw Him have passed along their testimony to us. When you trust Him, you receive resurrection life, eternal life (John 5:24); death can hold you no more.

We have a living hope (20–49). Jesus Christ will come

again, and the dead in Christ will be raised. We will have glorified bodies like Christ's body (1 John 3:1–3). Keep in mind that resurrection is not reconstruction. God does not reassemble the original body that has turned to dust. Like flowers and fruit from the planted seed, the glorified body is related to the "planted" body but different from it.

We have a living dynamic (50–58). We have no reason to give up because Jesus has conquered sin and death! If you really believe in the resurrection and return of Jesus, verse 58 will characterize your life. The best is yet to come, so let us give Him our best now.

❝In God's world, for those who are in earnest, there is no failure. No work truly done, no word earnestly spoken, no sacrifice freely made, was ever made in vain.**❞**

F. W. Robertson

---

1 CORINTHIANS 16

Love for the needy (1–4). These instructions concern the offering Paul was taking up from the churches to help the needy believers in Judea (Rom. 15:25–27). The principles involved may be applied to Christian giving in general: our giving should be voluntary, in proportion to God's blessing, systematic, and handled honestly.

Love for leaders (5–12). We have the privilege of encouraging God's work as we pray for His servants. Even men like Paul, Timothy, and Apollos needed the help and encouragement of God's people. Are you praying for leaders?

Love for the church (13–18). Love, steadfastness, and submission make for a strong church. When you have people who are devoted to the work of the Lord, people who refresh you in the Lord, God is going to bless. What a joy to be a part of a church family that ministers in love!

Love for Christ (19–24). "O Lord, come!" is a prayer that reveals Paul's daily anticipation of the return of the Lord. When he made his plans (vv. 5–8), he included the blessed hope. Do you love Him and love His appearing (2 Tim. 4:8)?

How Do You Pray?

"O Lord, come!" (1 Cor. 16:22) is in Aramaic *marana tha,* often seen as *maranatha. In the Lord's Prayer, we pray, "Your kingdom come" (Matt. 6:10); and the apostle John prayed, "Even so, come, Lord Jesus!" (Rev. 22:20). We should long for His coming, not just because we want to escape the trials of life but because we love Him and want to see Him face-to-face.*

SECOND CORINTHIANS

◆

The problems in the Corinthian church grew worse, and Paul had to make a painful visit to Corinth to confront the people causing the trouble (2 Cor. 2:1ff.). He then wrote a severe letter and sent it with Titus (2 Cor. 2:4–9; 7:8–12). After some delays, he and Titus finally met; and in response to the good news Titus brought from Corinth, Paul wrote this letter.

First, Paul described his ministry and explained why he had changed his plans (chaps. 1–7). It was a plea for *reconciliation.* Then he detailed the plans for taking up the love offering for the church in Judea (chaps. 8–9). It was a plea for *cooperation.* Because a group in the church questioned his authority, Paul concluded his letter defending his apostleship (chaps. 10–13). It was a plea for *appreciation* and obedience to the Word.

One key word in 2 Corinthians is *comfort* (encouragement), used in one form or another twenty-nine times. Yet there are many references to suffering, too. In this very personal letter Paul opens his heart and shares his deepest joys and sorrows. After all, Christians are human and must be honest in expressing their feelings.

2 CORINTHIANS 1

Christians need comfort. While trying to help the church, Paul experienced suffering so intense that he was almost ready to give up (vv. 8–9). God does not shelter His people from trials, not even gifted apostles who are doing His will. "Be kind," said John Watson, "for everyone you meet is fighting a battle."

Christians receive comfort. Your God is the "God of all comfort" (v. 3), and He will give you the grace you need when

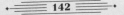

you need it. Sufferings are not accidents; they are divine appointments, and your Father is in complete control. You will find comfort in praying, in claiming the promises of the Word (vv. 18–20), and in having deeper fellowship with the Lord.

Christians share comfort. God's comfort is not *given*; it is *loaned*, and you are expected to pass it on to others. The pain you experience now will help you encourage others in their trials. When you suffer, avoid self-pity, for self-pity will make you a reservoir instead of a channel. If you fail to share God's comfort with others, your experience in the furnace will be wasted; and it is a tragic thing to waste your sufferings.

Blessed Be the Lord

What do 2 Corinthians 1:3, Ephesians 1:3, and 1 Peter 1:3 have in common? All three are doxologies, praising the Lord for what He does for His people. They deal with past, present, and future blessings in the Christian life. In your sufferings, take time to praise the Lord. It is good medicine for a hurting heart.

❝God does not comfort us to make us comfortable, but to make us comforters.❞

John Henry Jowett

2 CORINTHIANS 2

Feelings (1–5). From a heart of love touched with pain, Paul wrote a severe letter to the church, hoping to correct the problem. It brought grief to his dear friends, and that brought grief to Paul; but they disciplined the man who had caused the trouble. Paul was not afraid to share his feelings with others.

When you are out of touch with your feelings, you are out of touch with reality.

Forgiveness (6–11). When sinners truly repent, we should forgive them and reaffirm our love to them. Otherwise, they might become discouraged and give Satan an opportunity to accuse and attack (Rev. 12:10). Love does not condone sin, but it does cover sin when God has washed it away (James 5:20).

Fragrance (12–17). Paul described a Roman Triumph, the official parade given to a victorious general when he returned to Rome. The incense carried by the priests meant life to the Roman soldiers but death to the prisoners who would end up in the arena with the wild beasts. Christ has conquered, and we are privileged to march in His triumphal procession!

2 CORINTHIANS 3

The legalists who caused trouble in both Antioch and Jerusalem (Acts 15) had come to Corinth and enticed some of the believers into living by the law of Moses. Paul refuted their position by showing the wonders of the new covenant ministry. The background is Exodus 34:29–35.

It changes hearts (1–3). The law only reveals sin; it cannot renew the inner person. The Spirit wants to write a new version of His Word on your heart. Will you let Him?

It gives life (4–6). The law kills, but grace gives life and sustains that life. God's children have a living relationship with Him through the Spirit of life (Rom. 8:2).

It gets more and more glorious (7–16). The glory of the law is gone: the temple, the priesthood, the ceremonies, and the awesome revelations of God's power. But the glory of God's grace remains and grows more glorious (v. 18; Prov. 4:18).

It brings freedom (17–18). The law brings bondage (Acts 15:10), but grace gives glorious freedom that makes us more and more like Jesus Christ. Each day, you can have your own personal transfiguration as you worship the Lord and yield to the Spirit.

2 CORINTHIANS 4

The glory of salvation (1–6). Unlike the legalists who had invaded the church, Paul had nothing to hide. The Jewish reli-

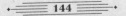

gious system veiled the gospel, but Paul sought to reveal the gospel. The image is taken from Genesis 1:1–3 and transferred from the old creation to the new creation (2 Cor. 5:17).

The glory of service (7–12). Paul paid a price for his ministry, but the legalists went about collecting honors (3:1). We are vessels; the treasure of the gospel life within is important. As vessels, we must be clean and available for His use (2 Tim. 2:20–21).

The glory of suffering (13–18). Jesus suffered and turned that suffering into glory; by faith, we can do the same thing. It is not wrong to care for the outward person, so long as you recognize that it is perishing. Concentrate on the inner person. It is the invisible that is imperishable. The best is yet to come!

"Lord, Thou knowest better than I know that I am growing older. Keep me from getting too talkative and thinking I must say something on every subject and on every occasion. Release me from craving to straighten out everybody's affairs. Teach me the glorious lesson that occasionally it is possible that I may be mistaken. Make me thoughtful, but not moody; helpful, but not bossy; Thou knowest, Lord, that what I want is a few friends at the end.**"**

---

2 CORINTHIANS 5

We know (1). This building is our new body that we will receive when we see the Lord (Phil. 3:20–21) because God saves the whole person (1 Cor. 15:42–58).

We groan (2–4). Creation is groaning and God's people also groan (Rom. 8:18–23), yearning for the Lord Jesus to come again. We do not want to die and leave our "houses"; we want

these bodies to be "clothed with" the glory of God from heaven (1 John 3:1–2). Paul longed to see Jesus come in his lifetime.

We are confident (5–8). God's Word gives us the truth about death and beyond, and God's Spirit guarantees that God's children will go to heaven. We claim this by faith and walk with confidence, and what peace it gives!

We aim to please Him (9–21). Paul's spiritual motivations for service include the judgment seat of Christ (vv. 9–11), the love of Christ (vv. 12–16), the power of the gospel (v. 17), and the commission of the Lord (vv. 18–21). What motivates you to do His will?

2 CORINTHIANS 6

Acceptance (1–2). Often those in the church who cause problems are people who have never truly been born again. They may think they are saved, but they are not. *Now* is the time to accept God's grace. Tomorrow may be too late.

Appreciation (3–13). It is easy to forget the sacrifices others have made so we can know the Lord. Paul never spoke about his sufferings unless his words helped to protect the ministry (11:16ff.). Do you take your church fellowship for granted? Have you thanked those who came before you and made it possible?

Agreement (14–18). Believers in the church were compromising with the world and not walking in a separated way (Ps. 1:1). God longs to have a closer fellowship with us, but He will not share the yoke with the world.

2 CORINTHIANS 7

Cleansing (1). It is one thing to ask God to cleanse you (Ps. 51:2, 7) and quite something else to cleanse yourself and put away the things that defile (Isa. 1:16). Separation sometimes demands surgery.

Comforting (2–7). The same people who give you joy can also cause you sorrow. When Titus reported that the church had disciplined the offender, the apostle was overjoyed. Have you ever been an answer to somebody's prayers as Titus was?

Clearing (8–11). If we are serious about repentance, we will do everything we can to clear things up. Remorse and regret

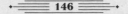

do not go far enough; there must be repentance followed by restitution.

Caring (12–16). Both Paul and Titus cared about the believers in Corinth, and this love finally won the day. You take a risk when you love others, for they may hurt you; but it is worth the risk to be like Jesus Christ and live a life of love.

| *True Repentance* | Regret *involves the mind primarily, and* remorse *involves the emotions. But* repentance *includes a change of mind, a hatred for sin, and a willingness to make things right. If the will is not touched, conviction has not gone deep enough.* |

---

2 CORINTHIANS 8—9

Chapters 8–9 focus on the offering Paul was taking for the needy believers in Judea. The Corinthian church had agreed to share in the collection but had been remiss in doing so. Paul reminded them of their promise and at the same time explained some principles of Christian giving.

It begins with surrender to the Lord (8:1–7). You cannot give your substance until you first give yourself (v. 5; Rom. 12:1–2). When you belong to the Lord, you start looking for opportunities to give instead of excuses not to give.

It is motivated by grace (8:8–9). Jesus was rich in heaven but became poor on earth (even to death on a cross!) that we might share His eternal riches. It was all by grace because *giving is a grace.* Law *commands,* but grace *consents* and does so joyfully.

It requires faith (8:10–15). The example of the manna (Exod. 16) shows that God always provides what we need. Paul also used the image of sowing to encourage generous giving (9:6). God's promises can be trusted.

It also requires faithfulness (8:16–24). Those who handle the Lord's money should be dedicated and faithful, making certain that everything is honest and honorable.

It is a testimony to others (9:1–5). A year before, the zeal of the Corinthians had stirred others to give; now Paul had to stir up the Corinthians! We must not give to be praised by people (Matt. 6:1–4), but we must also be good examples before others. If we make promises, we should keep them.

It must be done gladly (9:6–15). If you want spiritual enrichment from your giving (9:11), you must practice enjoyment and be glad for opportunities to give. Look at God's promises to faithful givers! How can you lose?

> **❝***For the Macedonian Christians, giving was not a chore but a challenge, not a burden but a blessing. Giving was not something to be avoided but a privilege to be desired.***❞**
>
> George Sweeting

---

2 CORINTHIANS 10

Satan seeks to blind minds to God's light (4:3–6), fortify minds against God's truth (vv. 1–6), and seduce minds from God's love (11:1–4). Paul gives some practical counsel for victory in spiritual warfare.

Be Christlike (1). Boldness must be balanced with meekness, for God's power is experienced in humility. Satan is our enemy, not people held by his power.

Use spiritual weapons (2–6). Paul may have had in mind Joshua's victory at Jericho (Josh. 6) when the walls came down because of Israel's faith. Read Ephesians 6:1–20, and be sure you are wearing the whole armor.

Keep your eyes on the Lord (7–11). That the Corinthians accused Paul of inconsistency gave Satan opportunity to work in their lives.

Accept the sphere of service God gives you (12–16). Every Christian soldier has a place to fill; if we are all following His orders, the church will win the battle.

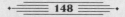

Seek God's glory alone (17–18). How can we boast in victories that God alone can give? Paul quoted Jeremiah 9:24 to remind us where the glory belongs.

2 CORINTHIANS 11

Paul compares himself to a father with obligations to his spiritual children.

Protection (1–4). Spiritual leaders must protect the church from false teachers who are like suitors trying to seduce the church from devotion to Christ. Beware losing your love for Christ and for those who helped you trust the Savior.

Provision (5–15). Paul had the right to receive financial support at Corinth, but he laid it aside and sacrificed for them in love. They did not appreciate it! But do you appreciate the sacrifices others make for you? Are you willing to sacrifice for others even when they do not thank you?

Suffering (16–33). Paul mentioned his sufferings only to defend the gospel and the authority of his ministry. The false teachers bragged about their triumphs, but Paul boasted about his trials.

❝The principle of sacrifice is that we choose to do or to suffer what apart from our love we should not choose to do or to suffer. When love is returned, this sacrifice is the most joyful thing in the world, and heaven is the life of joyful sacrifice. But in a selfish world it must be painful, and the pain is the source of triumph.**❞**

William Temple

---

2 CORINTHIANS 12

Permission. Just as God permitted Satan to test Job (Job 1—2) and Peter (Luke 22:31–34), so He permitted Satan to attack Paul. God wanted to keep Paul humble after his exciting visit to heaven. In the loving will of God, suffering has a purpose that can be fulfilled in no other way. Accept it, and it will become a heavenly blessing; fight it, and it will become a heavy burden.

Prayer. Like our Lord in Gethsemane (Matt. 26:44), Paul prayed three times for God to deliver him; but the Lord did not answer that prayer as Paul wanted. However, *God did meet the need* and gave His servant the grace he required. Paul did not simply make the best of it—he made the *most* of it! Grace can do that for you.

Perplexity. Paul was concerned more about the sins of the saints than about his own physical problems. Like a loving father, he wanted to go to Corinth and enjoy his dear children, but they were forcing him to discipline them. Yet, even discipline is an evidence of love (Heb. 12).

"We must form our estimate of men less from their
achievements and failures and more
from their sufferings.**"**

Dietrich Bonhoeffer

---

2 CORINTHIANS 13

As Paul planned his trip to Corinth, he envisioned the different kinds of people he would meet there.

The disobedient (1–4). Why would God's people want to disobey Him (12:20) and create problems for Paul and grief for the Lord, not to speak of problems for their church? Disobedient children must be dealt with, and Paul intended to be a faithful and loving father.

The disqualified (5–10). Some church members have never been born again, and that is why they create problems. Paul urges us to examine our hearts to be sure we are in the faith.

The devoted (11–14). These are the true brothers and sisters in the Lord, the set-apart ones (saints), the people who love one another and promote the peace and purity of the church. They are the mature ones in the fellowship who encourage spiritual growth.

To which group do you belong?

Solutions *Every local church problem can be solved by being humble and honest and by drawing on the spiritual resources listed in 2 Corinthians 13:14. Do you avail yourself of these riches? Are you a part of the problem or a part of the answer?*

GALATIANS
◆

The churches Paul founded in the Roman province of Galatia (Acts 13—14) were invaded by false teachers like those Paul had refuted in the Jerusalem Council (Acts 15). We call these people "Judaizers" because they tried to bring Christians into bondage to the law of Moses.

Paul wrote this letter to magnify God's grace in salvation and to explain the freedom of God's people because of that grace (Gal. 5:1). It opens with a *personal affirmation* (chaps. 1—2) as Paul explains how God delivered him from bondage through faith in Jesus Christ. He then gives a *doctrinal explanation* and shows the relationship between law and grace (chaps. 3—4). He closes with a *practical application* that tells you how to enjoy grace and freedom in your daily life (chaps. 5—6).

Christian freedom is the liberty to become all that you can in Jesus Christ; it is not the license to do whatever you please. The worst bondage you can experience is living for yourself and yielding to the desires of the old nature (Rom. 6). "We have freedom to do good or evil," wrote St. Francis de Sales, "yet to make choice of evil, is not to use, but to abuse our freedom." Christ did not free us to be our own; He freed us to be His and His alone.

GALATIANS 1

To Paul, the gospel was much more than a message he preached: it was a miracle he had experienced (vv. 1-5). The gospel is "the power of God to salvation" (Rom. 1:16) and it brings freedom. Christ died "that He might deliver us" (v. 4). When Paul trusted Christ, he became a free man. The shackles of sin and legalistic religion were broken!

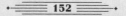

But the gospel was also a treasure that Paul guarded (vv. 6–17). Paul did not invent the gospel or learn it from others; God gave it to him (1 Cor. 15:1–11). *There is no other gospel.* To add to this message, take from it, or substitute another message is to destroy it. No wonder Paul attacked those who attacked the gospel; when you lose the gospel, you lose everything.

The gospel is a tie that binds God's people together (vv. 18–24). Saul the enemy became Paul the brother, and he was able to fellowship with people he once had persecuted. Christians may disagree on minor matters of interpretation and organization, but they agree on the message of the gospel.

> **❝**The gospel is neither a discussion nor a debate. It is an announcement.**❞**
>
> Paul S. Rees

GALATIANS 2

The runner (1–5). Paul saw himself as a man running a race, and he was sure he was on the right track and headed for the right goal. The Judaizers were trying to move the church into bondage and get them on a detour (5:7; Acts 15).

The steward (6–10). God has committed the gospel to His people, and we must guard it and share it with others. God is not looking for popular celebrities; He is looking for faithful stewards (1 Cor. 4:1–2).

The watchman (11–13). Paul was not afraid to confront the apostle Peter when Peter moved away from the truth of the gospel. "Eternal vigilance is the price of liberty!" said Wendell Phillips, and that applies to our spiritual liberty as well.

The destroyer (14–21). Jesus destroyed the law by fulfilling it (Matt. 5:17–20). His death tore the temple veil (Luke 23:44–45) and removed the wall between Jews and Gentiles (Eph. 2:14–18). To go back to Moses is to rebuild what Jesus tore down and say that He did not really save us when we trusted Him.

> *"Whitefield and Wesley might preach the gospel better than I do, but they cannot preach a better gospel."*
>
> Charles Spurgeon

GALATIANS 3

Examination (1–14). It does us good to examine ourselves to make sure our spiritual experience is valid (2 Cor. 13:5). Do you have the Spirit living within? (See Rom. 8:9.) If you began in the Spirit (which is the only way to begin), are you trying to continue in the power of the flesh? Like Abraham, were you saved by faith; and are you now, like Abraham, walking by faith?

Explanation (15–25). The Judaizers wanted the Galatians to go back to Moses, but that was not far enough. *We must go back to Abraham where the promise started.* The law did not annul the promise; the law was given to reveal sin and prepare the way for Christ to come and fulfill the promise. The law is a tutor, not a savior; a mirror, not a cleanser.

Exhortation (26–29). Beware! A false gospel robs you of salvation and of membership in the family of God where all believers are one in Christ. It robs you of your spiritual riches as an heir of the promise. Are you rejoicing in the freedom you have in Christ?

GALATIANS 4

Are you a child of God through faith in Jesus Christ? Then you are also an heir, and all of Christ's riches are yours (Eph. 1:3)! A child must wait until maturity to inherit the family wealth, but God's children can have His wealth now (Phil. 4:19).

Are you a child of God through faith in Jesus Christ? Then you are free! A child is in bondage and must be guarded by adults, but a grown son or daughter enjoys freedom. To live under Law is to be a slave, and God wants His children to enjoy their freedom in Christ.

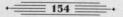

Are you a child of God through faith in Jesus Christ? Then you can become like Him as you yield to the Spirit (v. 19; 2 Cor. 3:18).

Are you a child of God through faith in Jesus Christ? Then your citizenship is secure in heaven because you are a child of promise (vv. 21–31; Gen. 16). You were born free!

Freedom in Christ

An allegory is a narrative in which people and events teach deeper lessons. John Bunyan's Pilgrim's Progress is a classic example. Paul used Genesis 16 to illustrate your freedom in Christ. Hagar is the law, while Sarah stands for God's grace. Ishmael was born after the flesh (your first birth), while Isaac was born by the power of God (the new birth). Abraham represents faith, so Isaac was born "by grace [Sarah] . . . through faith [Abraham]" (Eph. 2:8). The Judaizers wanted to bring Hagar back again, but she was sent away because law and grace cannot coexist. Like Hagar, the law was a servant that had a temporary ministry. Once the Son arrived, that ministry was fulfilled.

GALATIANS 5

Are you standing free (1)? Your freedom in Christ is a costly thing, for it cost Jesus His life. In Him, you stand free; the yoke of the law has been removed (Acts 15:6–11).

Are you falling (4)? To fall from grace does not mean to lose one's salvation. It means to move out of the sphere of grace into the sphere of law. It means to substitute regulations for a personal relationship with the Lord.

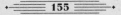

Are you running on course (7)? Or has false teaching gotten you on a detour?

Are you being leavened (9)? Jesus used leaven to picture sin (Matt. 16:6–12). Like yeast, false teaching is introduced quietly, it grows secretly, and soon it affects every part of your life.

Are you serving others (13)? Freedom brings with it the responsibility to serve. Love motivates us to fulfill the law of God (Rom. 13:8–14).

Are you walking in the Spirit (16)? Life, not law, changes behavior; and as you yield to the Spirit, Christ's life is manifest in the fruit of the Spirit.

Law works by compulsion from without, but grace works by compassion from within.

❝*Every time we say, 'I believe in the Holy Spirit,' we mean that we believe there is a living God able and willing to enter human personality and change it.***❞**

J. B. Phillips

GALATIANS 6

See others humbly (1–2). Your response to another's fall reveals your own walk, whether it is spiritual or not. Pride will make it impossible for you to help the fallen, but humility will bring blessing to you and to them.

See yourself honestly (3–5). Do you use somebody's fall to make yourself look better? Or do you know yourself, accept yourself, and seek to please God alone?

See your leaders appreciatively (6–10). When you give to others whose ministry blesses you, you are sowing seed that will bear fruit. When you use your resources for sinful purposes, you sow to the flesh and will reap a sad harvest.

See the Cross clearly (11–18). The false teachers wanted the world's praise, so they avoided the Cross; but the true believer will glory in the Cross, even if it means suffering the world's enmity.

Faithfully Restore Them

The word translated "restore" in Galatians 6:1 also means "to set a broken bone." How gentle and loving we must be when we seek to help fallen brothers or sisters, for what we do will affect them and the body of Christ.

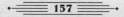

EPHESIANS

◆

On his second missionary journey, Paul visited Ephesus and left Aquila and Priscilla there (Acts 18:19–21). He returned to Ephesus two years later and ministered for three years, reaching the whole province of Asia with the gospel (Acts 19). Some years later when Paul was a prisoner in Rome (3:1; 4:1; 6:20), he wrote this letter to the believers in Ephesus.

One major theme of Ephesians is that God is at work in this world, through His church, putting things together (1:10). In the first three chapters, Paul explains this as a work of redemption (chap. 1), resurrection (2:1–10), and reconciliation (2:11–3:21). In chapters 4–6, Paul states the responsibilities of believers in the light of God's great purpose. Note the emphasis on the word *walk*.

Ephesus was an important city and boasted of being custodian of the temple of Diana, one of the seven wonders of the ancient world. The city was devoted to idolatry, which explains why Paul had so much to say about defeating the devil (6:10ff.).

The Ephesian letter shows the balance in the Christian life between doctrine (chaps. 1–3) and duty (chaps. 4–6), divine sovereignty and human responsibility. We do not obey God so that He will give us His grace; we obey Him in response to grace already given.

EPHESIANS 1

Salvation is of God. Man does not save himself, for "salvation is of the LORD" (Jon. 2:9). You receive spiritual blessings from the Father (vv. 1–6), the Son (vv. 7–12), and the Spirit (vv. 13–14); and in Jesus Christ, you have all you need for life and service.

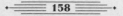

Salvation is all of grace. Paul emphasizes this point throughout the letter, especially in 2:1–10. Grace is God's favor bestowed on people who do not and cannot deserve it.

Salvation is for God's glory. God saves sinners not to solve their problems but to bring glory to Himself (vv. 6, 12, 14; 3:21). The church will glorify Him for all eternity!

Salvation reveals God's greatness (15–23). Ask God to open your spiritual eyes to see the greatness of His power. Jesus is alive and has conquered every enemy! You may draw on His power to meet every need in life.

Praying in His Will

The two prayers in Ephesians complement each other. Ephesians 1:15–23 focuses on knowing what God has done for you in Christ, while 3:14–21 emphasizes experiencing His blessings. The first is for enlightenment; the second is for enablement. For other prison prayers of Paul, see Philippians 1:9–11 and Colossians 1:9–12. You may use these prayers for yourself and know that you are praying in the will of God.

EPHESIANS 2

From death to life. Lost sinners are not simply sick people needing help; they are dead people needing life. The Son of God died that we might receive life through faith in Him (John 5:24).

From bondage to freedom. Lost sinners are in bondage to the world, the flesh, and the devil (vv. 1–3) and cannot free themselves. In Christ, you have true freedom (John 12:31–32; Gal. 1:4; 5:24). Now God is working in you and through you to accomplish His great purposes (v. 10).

From the tomb to the throne. God did not give you life and leave you in the cemetery. He lifted you up to sit on the throne with His victorious Son!

From separation to reconciliation. In Jesus Christ, believing Jews and Gentiles are now one; the barriers have been removed. Believers are members of one body, citizens of one holy nation, and living stones in one temple (1 Pet. 2:1–10).

All of this is of God, His marvelous love (v. 4), and His grace and kindness (v. 7). No wonder Paul opened this letter with a doxology (1:3)!

EPHESIANS 3

A purpose. "For this reason" (vv. 1, 14) refers to what Paul wrote at the end of chapter 2, the building of the church. That was the purpose behind his praying and his ministering. Jesus said, "I will build My church" (Matt. 16:18), but He uses people to help get the job done. Is the building of the church your motivation to pray and serve?

A parenthesis. The word *Gentiles* (v. 1) put Paul in prison (Acts 22:21). God gave him a special commission to evangelize the Gentiles and to explain to both Jews and Gentiles God's "mystery" (sacred secret): in Christ, believing Jews and Gentiles are one and share the same spiritual riches. As He builds His church in this world, God is putting things together. Are you helping Him?

A prayer. This prayer is for spiritual vision, to see and lay hold of the greatness of God's love and power. God wants you to be concerned about "the whole building" (2:21), "the whole family" (3:15), "the whole body" (4:16), and "all the saints" (v. 18). Is narrowness in your life leading to shallowness and weakness?

EPHESIANS 4

To "give place to the devil" (v. 27) is to allow unconfessed sin in your life that gives Satan an opportunity to take over. Some sins to avoid are discussed here.

Disunity (1–13). Believers are "all one in Christ Jesus" (Gal. 3:28), but we must endeavor to make that spiritual unity a

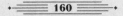

practical reality in our daily lives. Satan uses people who like to have their own way.

Immaturity (14–16). Spiritual birth must lead to spiritual growth as we become more like Jesus Christ (1 Pet. 1:22—2:3). If we are maturing in Christ, we will show it by being able to speak the truth in love. Satan is a liar and a murderer (John 8:44) and has a difficult time being successful when believers practice truth and love.

Impurity (17–32). You have been set free from the old life, so why live in those old sins anymore? Anything evil from the old life that is brought into the new life will give the devil a beachhead. Paul names such things as lying, losing your temper, stealing, corrupt speech, bitterness, and an unforgiving spirit. These sins invite Satan into your life, and they hurt you, harm the church, and grieve the Spirit of God. Is it worth it?

EPHESIANS 5

As he encourages us to live godly lives, Paul takes us to *the temple* (vv. 1–7) and reminds us of the sacrifice Jesus made for us. If we walk in love, our lives will be living sacrifices (Rom. 12:1–2; Phil. 2:17), fragrant to the Lord (John 12:1–8). Sin is ugly and a stench in God's nostrils (Isa. 3:24).

Then Paul goes to *the field* (vv. 8–14) and reminds us that walking in the light produces spiritual fruit (Gal. 5:22–23). If we walk in the light, we cannot have fellowship with the darkness (2 Cor. 6:14–18).

He takes us to *the marketplace* (vv. 15–17) and exhorts us to be like good merchants who know how to buy up an opportunity. When you walk in wisdom, you use your time wisely.

Then we follow him to *the banqueting hall* (vv. 18–21) and learn to walk in the Spirit (Gal. 5:16–26) and be joyful, thankful, and submissive to one another.

Paul's last visit is to *the home* (vv. 22–33) where he uses marriage as a picture of the relationship between Christ and the church. Christ *loved* us and died for us, but today He *loves* us and cares for us. This intimate life is pictured in the Song of Solomon and can be a reality for all who will yield to Him.

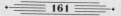

Under the Spirit's Influence

To be "filled with" means "to be controlled by" (Luke 4:28; 5:26). On the day of Pentecost, the believers were filled with the Holy Spirit and were accused of being drunk (Acts 2:13). Just as a drunk is influenced by alcohol, so a believer should be controlled by the Spirit. However, there are important differences. The drunk loses self-control, but the Spirit gives the believer self-control (Gal. 5:23). The drunk has an artificial happiness that does not last, while the Spirit-filled believer has a deep joy in the Lord. Drunken people do stupid things that hurt others and bring them embarrassment, but Spirit-filled believers help others and live to the glory of God.

EPHESIANS 6

Spirit-filled Christians will manifest Christlikeness in the home (vv. 1–4), on the job (vv. 5–9), and on the battlefield (vv. 10–20). If we do not learn to obey at home, we are not likely to be obedient on the job or in the army of the Lord. Likewise, if we have not learned to *take* orders, we will not be too successful at *giving* orders, either as parents or as employers.

The danger in the home is parents who are *authoritarian* but do not exercise loving spiritual *authority*. The danger on the job is the employee who is a clock-watcher and does not obey from the heart, and the "boss" who forgets that he is second in command and must one day give an account to the Lord.

The danger on the battlefield is that we do not take the enemy seriously and therefore fail to put on all of the armor. By

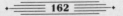

faith, you put on the armor through prayer, which must be done at the beginning of every day. Never underestimate the strategy and strength of the devil.

"Stand Up, Stand Up for Jesus"

> *"Stand up, stand up for Jesus,*
> *Stand in His strength alone;*
> *The arm of flesh will fail you,*
> *You dare not trust your own.*
> *Put on the gospel armor,*
> *Each piece put on with prayer;*
> *Where duty calls or danger,*
> *Be never wanting there."*
>
> George Duffield

PHILIPPIANS

Founded on Paul's second missionary journey (Acts 16), the church at Philippi was a source of real joy to him. Hearing that Paul was a prisoner in Rome, the Philippian believers sent a special love offering; and in this letter, Paul wrote to express his thanks. He also wrote to explain why Epaphroditus, their messenger, had been delayed and to encourage the believers to work together to bring unity to the church.

The overriding theme of the letter is Jesus Christ and the ministry of the gospel. Christ is the message of our ministry (chap. 1) as well as the model (chap. 2), the motive (chap. 3), and the means (chap. 4). The theme of joy is also woven throughout the letter. Despite his difficult circumstances, Paul rejoiced in the Lord and urged his readers to do so. After all, the joy of the Lord is the strength of Christian service (Neh. 8:10).

PHILIPPIANS 1

Paul wrote, "For to me, to live is Christ" (v. 21). But he did more than *write* that statement; he *lived* it. Jesus Christ is mentioned eighteen times in this chapter and is seen involved in many aspects of Paul's life.

His friends (1–11). Paul loved the saints in Philippi; he thought about them, prayed for them, and longed to see them. Christ made this fellowship possible.

His circumstances (12–18). He was a prisoner not of Rome but of Jesus Christ, and his chains were "in Christ" (v. 13). Paul was practicing Romans 8:28—and it worked! Do you think first of Christ when circumstances are difficult?

His future (19–26). Paul's life was in danger; if he lost the trial, he could be killed as an enemy of Rome. But when Christ

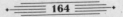

is your life, death is not your enemy; and you have the assurance of being with Christ when life ends.

His enemies (27–30). When you suffer, you suffer for Christ's sake; and you need not fear your enemies. The vital thing is that God's people unite in Christ and oppose the enemy, not one another!

Alive to Christ	*"Life is what we are alive to," wrote Maltbie Babcock. Sports fans may be weary, but if they hear of an athletic event taking place, they come alive and want to attend. Hungry people are alive to the mention of food, and avid shoppers come alive at the announcement of a sale. So Christians are alive to all pertaining to Jesus Christ, for Christ is their very life.*

PHILIPPIANS 2

Look out (1–11). Christ is the model for Christian life and service because He thought first of others, not of Himself. Do you look out for the interests of others, or do you think only of yourself? Do you have the servant attitude of Jesus Christ, willing to sacrifice for others? Will you empty yourself that others might be filled?

Work out (12–16). As you yield to the Lord, He works in and you work out; in this way, you fulfill His plan for your life (Eph. 2:10). God cannot shine *through* you until He works *in* you, so let Him have His way. You are a light in a dark world, a runner holding forth the living Word to a dead world.

Poured out (17–30). The image is that of the drink offering, poured out on the altar (Num. 15:1–10). Paul was willing to pour out his very life for the sake of the Lord and the church, and to do it *joyfully*. Timothy and Epaphroditus had the same attitude of service and sacrifice, giving themselves for others.

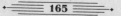

> **❝**I used to think that God's gifts were on shelves one
> above the other, and that the taller we grew in
> Christian character the more easily we could reach
> them. I now find that God's gifts are on shelves one
> beneath the other and that it is not a question
> of growing taller but of stooping lower.**❞**
>
> F. B. Meyer

PHILIPPIANS 3

Rejoicing (1). If you cannot rejoice in your circumstances, you can always rejoice in the Lord who controls your circumstances. Fix your attention on Him. He may not change your situation, but He will change you; and that is even better.

Counting (2–11). What is important to you? Do you feel you have made sacrifices to follow the Lord? Paul did not feel he had lost anything worthwhile by trusting Christ. Instead, he gained everything really worth having.

Reaching (12–16). Christians are like runners who refuse to look around or look back but keep running with their eyes on the goal. To look back at past successes or failures, or to look around to see what others are doing or saying, is to invite defeat. Heed Hebrews 12:1–2.

Weeping (17–19). This is the only mention of tears in a letter devoted to joy. Paul wept over professed Christians who lived to please themselves. Instead of having the mind of Christ, they thought like the world, and these people are with us today.

Looking (20–21). Paul looked up and eagerly anticipated the return of the Lord. Christ had taken care of his past (v. 13), and He would also take care of his future. And as for Paul's present, his confidence was knowing that "He is able!" (v. 21).

PHILIPPIANS 4

The message of our ministry is the gospel of Christ (chap. 1). The model for our ministry is the example of Christ (chap. 2). The motive for our ministry is the reward of Christ (chap. 3). The means of our ministry is the provision of Christ (chap. 4).

He provides unity when we disagree with our fellow Christians (vv. 1–5), and peace when we are prone to worry (vv. 6–9). If we pray as we ought to pray and think as we ought to think, the peace of God will guard us, and the God of peace will go with us.

He provides the power we need for life and service (vv. 10–13) and the material needs we have as well (vv. 14–20). Paul did not have a wealthy organization giving him support, but he did have a great God who enabled generous friends to meet his needs. Paul saw their gift as a fragrant sacrifice to the Lord (v. 18), and he rejoiced in the Lord for what they did.

◆

| *Reach Your Potential* | *Charles W. Koller affirmed that through Christ you can be what you ought to be (Phil. 4:11), do what you ought to do (v. 13), and have what you ought to have (v. 19), all to the glory of God.* |

◆

COLOSSIANS

◆

Epaphras, one of Paul's converts, founded the church in Colosse (1:7; 4:12–13); Paul had never been there personally (2:1). While imprisoned in Rome, Paul heard that false doctrines were being introduced in the church, so he wrote this letter to warn the believers and to establish them in the faith.

The key theme is the preeminence of Christ (1:18) because the false teachers made Christ one of several emanations from God. They mixed Christian truth with their doctrines of Jewish legalism and Oriental mysticism. Colossians is the perfect answer to the so-called New Age movement today, for Paul affirms that in Jesus Christ believers are complete and have the fullness of God available to them (2:9–10).

Chapters 1—2 are doctrinal and present Jesus Christ as the preeminent Creator, Savior, and Lord. Chapters 3—4 are practical and show how the believer works out the preeminence of Christ in daily living. Because the epistles to the Ephesians and Colossians were written about the same time, you will see parallels; but Ephesians emphasizes the body (the church), while Colossians emphasizes the Head of the body (Jesus Christ). The letters complement each other.

COLOSSIANS 1

The hope before you (1–12). These people were going to heaven! They had heard the Word and trusted the Savior, and they had given evidence of their faith by their love for God and God's people. God qualified them (v. 12); they did not save themselves.

The hope beneath you (13–23). Hope is a foundation on

which you stand when all around you is shaking. The city of Colosse was located in an earthquake area, so Paul's admonition was especially meaningful to them (v. 23). The false teachers wanted the saints to shift their foundation, but Paul pointed the church to Jesus Christ: Savior (vv. 13–14), eternal God (v. 15), Creator (vv. 16–17), and Head of the church (v. 18). What a perfect foundation for your hope!

The hope within you (24–29). Heaven is more than a destination; it is a motivation because Christ lives within. It is a living hope (1 Pet. 1:3) that affects how we think and act all day long. Because Christ is within us, we need not fear what is ahead.

Firstborn

"Firstborn over all creation" (Col. 1:15) does not mean Jesus was a created being and not eternal God, nor does "firstborn from the dead" (v. 18) mean He was the first one raised from the dead. Firstborn is a term of honor and means "the highest, of first rank and importance." Jesus was prior to all creation (John 1:1–3) and is the highest in creation. He is the highest of all who were raised from the dead (Rev. 1:17–18).

Thanksgiving

Note the emphasis on thanksgiving in Colossians (1:3, 12; 2:7; 3:17; 4:2). The more wonderful we see Jesus to be, the more we will be grateful to God for Him and His blessings.

COLOSSIANS 2

Paul wrote to the Colossians, "You must never allow anyone to come between you and Christ. In Him is all wisdom and knowledge (v. 3) and all the fullness of God (v. 9), and you are complete in Him (v. 10). Why accept a substitute?"

Let no one deceive you (4). Religious systems seem so inviting, and their leaders are so persuasive. But if you follow them, you will substitute man's ideas for God's truth.

Let no one cheat you (8). Here the thief is man-made philosophy and tradition, pleasing to the world but rejected by the Lord. If you have all fullness in Christ, why substitute man's empty philosophies?

Let no one judge you (16). Legalism is the robber here (v. 21), stealing your liberty in Christ and making you live by religious regulations instead of by God's grace.

Let no one defraud you (18). Here the culprit is religious mysticism that replaces spiritual nourishment from Christ with empty (but exciting) religious experiences.

You have in Christ all that you need. Beware substitutes!

❝*The greatest philosophy ever produced does not come within a thousand leagues of the fathomless profundity of our Lord's statements, e.g., 'Learn of Me, for I am meek and lowly in heart.'*❞

Oswald Chambers

COLOSSIANS 3

Having laid the doctrinal foundation, Paul now makes the personal application, for truth is something to *live* as well as to *learn*.

Put to death (1–7). In Christ, you have died to the old life and been raised to a new life (Rom. 6:1–14; Eph. 2:1–10), so make the new life the focus of your attention. Set your mind on it; seek to experience all that you have in Christ.

Put off (8–9). Like Lazarus (John 11:44), you must get rid of the graveclothes that belong to the old life. By faith, put off the old sins that bound you; Christ has set you free.

Put on (10–25). God wants you to wear the graceclothes, not the graveclothes! If your focus is on things heavenly, you will obey God in things on earth, especially in your relationships with others.

Filled with the Word	*Colossians 3:16—4:1 parallels Ephesians 5:18—6:9, except that the emphasis here is on being filled with the Word of God. When the Word controls your life, you will be joyful (3:16), thankful (3:17), and submissive (3:18—4:1), and these are the same characteristics of the Spirit-filled Christian as explained in Ephesians 5:18—6:9. To be filled with the Spirit of God means to be controlled by the Word of God.*

COLOSSIANS 4

Praying (2–4, 12–13). Prayer involves a persevering will, an alert mind, and a grateful heart; and our requests should be specific and related to the ministry of the Word. Paul asked not for an open prison door but for an open door of ministry (1 Cor. 16:9; 2 Cor. 2:12; Rev. 3:7–8).

Witnessing (5–6). The unsaved are outside the family of God, and it is our task to bring them in. Effective witness involves walking wisely, being alert to every opportunity, and being careful in what we say and how we say it (1 Pet. 3:15–17).

Informing (7–9). Paul did not hesitate to share his needs with others, because he depended on their prayer support (Rom. 15:30; Eph. 6:19; Phil. 1:19; 1 Thess. 5:25; Philem. 22). Do you pray for Christian leaders in places of importance? They need it!

Serving (10–18). Paul names six men who were working at his side and encouraging him in the Lord. Even an apostle cannot get the job done alone, and how grateful he was for the saints serving faithfully in Colosse!

Servants of the Lord	*Years before, Paul had refused to serve with John Mark (Acts 15:36–41) because Mark had left the work (Acts 13:5–13); but now Paul and John Mark were friends and colaborers. Luke had been a part of Paul's team since their ministry at Philippi (Acts 16:10). Alas, Demas would eventually forsake Paul and the Lord (Philem. 24; 2 Tim. 4:10). Do you pray for the men and women who serve with Christian leaders, that they might be faithful to the Lord?*

THE THESSALONIAN EPISTLES

---◆---

Acts 17:1-15 records the founding of the church in Thessalonica. Paul ministered there a short time, possibly only a month; but the Lord did a great work, and the witness of the church was known far and wide.

Paul had to leave the city and was not able to return, so he sent Timothy to see how things were going. Paul wrote the first letter from Corinth (Acts 18:5) in response to Timothy's report (3:6). He wanted to encourage the saints in their Christian walk and assure them of his love and concern.

The second letter was written a few months later to encourage the church to be steadfast in the midst of persecution. Some of the people thought the "day of the Lord" had come, so Paul dealt with that theme as well. Both letters emphasize the coming of Christ and the practical effect it should have on our lives.

FIRST THESSALONIANS

—◆—

1 THESSALONIANS 1

Paul's description of the believers in Thessalonica suggests that they typify an ideal congregation. Ask yourself these questions.

Are others thankful for me (1–4)? Paul was grateful for their faith, hope, and love, and that these Christian qualities revealed themselves in work, labor, and patience. Can others tell that we belong to God? Are they thankful for our spiritual growth?

◆————————————

Jesus' Return	Every chapter in 1 Thessalonians ends with a reference to the return of Jesus Christ, and that truth is applied to daily living. An eager looking for His return is an evidence of salvation (1:9–10), a motivation for soul winning (2:17–20), and an encouragement for holy living (3:11–13). This truth is a comfort in sorrow (4:18) and a stimulus to have more confidence in the Lord (5:23–24).

————————————◆

Is God's power seen in my life (5–7)? This comes when you receive the Word of God by faith and allow the Spirit of God to minister to your heart. It also involves suffering for the Lord and letting Him give you His joy.

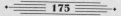

Do I make it easier for others to talk about Jesus (8–10)? Some believers are such poor examples as Christians that their lives give unbelievers an excuse for rejecting Christ. But the Thessalonian Christians made it easy for Paul to preach the gospel! Their testimony had gone before him and met him wherever he went.

1 THESSALONIANS 2

Faithfulness (1–6). Paul's sufferings in Philippi might have made him hesitate to minister in Thessalonica, but he was a steward who wanted to be faithful to the Lord. His message and motive were pure, and God blessed his ministry. It is better to be approved by God and suffer than to be applauded by men and prosper. When you feel like quitting, keep going (1 Cor. 4:2).

Gentleness (7–9). Young believers need a spiritual parent to lovingly nurture them in the Lord. Paul's ministry was motivated by love, not by pride or the desire for material gain.

Blamelessness (10–12). How important it is to be good examples before young believers! Children do what we do, not what we say. Does your example as a Christian make it easier for others to grow?

Eagerness (13–16). These people had an appetite for the Word of God, and that helped them to grow (Jer. 15:16; 1 Pet. 2:2). When they heard God's Word, they eagerly welcomed it and put it to work immediately.

Hopefulness (17–20). Paul hoped to visit his beloved friends again; but even if they did not meet on earth, he would meet them at the coming of the Lord. When Jesus comes, will you rejoice in His presence because of people you have influenced for Christ?

1 THESSALONIANS 3

What should you do when people you love need your help, but you cannot go to them? The new believers in Thessalonica desperately needed Paul's ministry, but he was not able to return to help them. So, he did what he could.

First, he sent Timothy to minister to the church. If you cannot go, try to get somebody qualified to go in your place.

Then, he prayed for them (v. 10) because prayer is not limited by time or place. Your prayers for your loved ones will do more good than you realize, so keep praying.

Paul encouraged them by writing them at least two letters. His great concern was not their comfort or safety but their faith (vv. 2, 5–7, 10), their love (v. 12), and their obedience to the Lord (v. 13). Perhaps today you could write a letter or send a card to someone who needs your encouragement.

1 THESSALONIANS 4

"More and more" should be the desire of the dedicated Christian (vv. 1, 10).

More holiness (1–8). Your body belongs to God, and His will is that you use it for holy purposes. Christ purchased your body (1 Cor. 6:18–20), the Spirit dwells in your body (v. 8), and the Father has called you to holy living (v. 7). Disobey and the penalties are great!

More love (9–10). You are taught to love by the Father (1 John 4:19), the Son (John 13:34), and the Spirit (Rom. 5:5). Love is one mark of the true believer (1 John 3:14).

More quietness (11–12). Because they expected the Lord to return any day, some believers had quit their jobs and become idlers and meddlers (2 Thess. 3:6–15). What kind of testimony would this be to the lost?

More hope (13–18). Christians sorrow because God made us to weep; but it is not the hopeless sorrow of the world. Jesus is coming again, and that means reunion and eternal rejoicing!

1 THESSALONIANS 5

False peace (1–11). The "day of the Lord" is that time when God will pour out His wrath on the world. God's people have been saved from wrath, so they need not worry (v. 9; 1:10); but the lost world will be caught at a time when they think they are secure. To be ready for Christ's coming, God's people must be sober and live in the light.

Family peace (12–22). The local church fellowship should reflect God's peace; and it will if God's people obey authority, minister to one another, and submit to the Spirit of God.

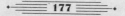

Verse 21 emphasizes the positive and verse 22 the negative, and both are important.

Faithful peace (23–28). Holiness and peace go together (Isa. 32:17), for the God who quiets the heart also cleanses the heart (James 3:17). A disturbed heart is sometimes evidence of unconfessed sin. God is faithful; let Him bring purity and peace to your heart.

Welcome the Spirit's Ministry

"Do not quench the Spirit" (1 Thess. 5:19) is an admonition to Christians not to resist and reject the ministry of the Spirit. The image is that of fire (Isa. 34:4; Acts 2:3; Rev. 4:5). Just as fire brings light, heat, and cleansing, so the Spirit enlightens, enables, and purifies His people. Paul reminded Timothy to "stir up the gift of God" (2 Tim. 1:6), which means "get the fire burning again." Are you allowing the fire to go out on the altar of your life (Lev. 6:9, 12)?

I have noticed this, that when a man is full of the Holy Ghost, he is the very last man to be complaining of other people. He loves everybody too tenderly. He loves even a cold church, and is anxious to lift them up and bring them to a kinder feeling and sympathy.

D. L. Moody

SECOND THESSALONIANS

◆

2 THESSALONIANS 1

Along with persecutions on the outside, the church was facing problems on the inside. Some people were suffering great trials for their faith. Others had quit working and were idlers. Still others were harboring the wrong idea that they were experiencing the "day of the Lord." Paul wrote this letter to encourage the suffering (chap. 1), enlighten the confused (chap. 2), and warn the careless (chap. 3).

In times of trial, the essential thing is your faith (v. 3). God will see you through, so trust His promises. Remember that others are watching you and you can encourage them (v. 4). You may be tempted to fight back, but leave that to the Lord (vv. 5–9).

“No pain, no palm; no thorns, no throne; no gall, no glory; no cross, no crown.”

William Penn

The lost will be eternally separated from God's glory (v. 9), while the saved will bring glory to the Lord (v. 10). Meanwhile, be sure that God is glorified by your life today (vv. 11–12).

2 THESSALONIANS 2

Satan wants to shake the saints and make them lose their confidence, and one of his chief weapons is deception. Some-

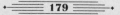

one claimed to have a letter from Paul saying that the day of the Lord was present, and others said they had messages through the Spirit (1 Thess. 5:21). The believers forgot what Paul had taught them (v. 5), so they were trapped by the lies of the enemy.

The "times and seasons" of God's prophetic plan are in God's hands (Acts 1:6–8), and He has everything in control. A sequence of events is sketched here to assure us that the church is destined for salvation and not judgment (v. 13; 1 Thess. 1:10; 5:9). The Spirit of God in this world is keeping God's program on schedule.

Beware "prophets" who contradict what God has already said in His Word (v. 15). If you stand on the Word, you will not fall for the devil's lies. God's people can face the future with assurance, hope, and comfort because of the unfailing grace of God (vv. 13–17).

2 THESSALONIANS 3

Conflict (1–2). Anyone who seeks to live for the Lord will have enemies (2 Tim. 3:12). The weapon we use is prayer, and the purpose for which we pray is the sharing of the Word of God (Col. 4:2–3). Not everybody in the church at Thessalonica was devoted to the Lord, but Paul still asked for their prayers.

❝*Work is not primarily a thing one does to live, but the thing one lives to do. It is, or should be, the full expression of the worker's faculties, the thing in which he finds spiritual, mental and bodily satisfaction, and the medium in which he offers himself to God.*❞

Dorothy L. Sayers

Confidence (3–5). God's faithfulness to us is the basis for our faithfulness to Him. If we love Him, we will keep His Word, and we will be patient in times of trial.

Command (6–15). The word *command* (vv. 4, 6, 10, 12) means "a military order." Some of the Christian soldiers in the church were breaking rank and disobeying orders, and Paul had to admonish them. Those who cannot work must be cared for by others, but those who *will not* work must be disciplined. Never let the bad example of others keep you from being a good example.

FIRST TIMOTHY

◆

Paul's trial in Rome came out in his favor, and he was released. It is likely he went to Colosse to visit Philemon (Philem. 22). He may have written 1 Timothy from Colosse or from Philippi.

The child of a mixed marriage (Acts 16:1), Timothy was raised in a godly home (2 Tim. 1:5; 3:15) and came to know Christ through Paul's ministry (1 Tim. 1:2). Paul added him to his team at Lystra (Acts 16:1–3) and made him one of his special assistants (Phil. 2:19–22). Timothy eventually was sent to pastor the church in Ephesus (1 Tim. 1:3).

First Timothy is a ministerial letter, telling pastors and people how they should conduct themselves in the local assembly (3:15). Paul stresses preaching the truth (chaps. 1, 4), praying (chap. 2), and appointing qualified leaders (chap. 3). He closes by giving counsel on how to minister to various kinds of people in the church (chaps. 5–6).

1 TIMOTHY 1

The work in Ephesus was not easy, and Timothy wanted a new assignment; but Paul urged him to stay where he was and get the job done (1:3). The next time you want to abandon your assigned place, consider the arguments Paul gave Timothy for staying where he was.

For the work's sake (1–11). What Paul warned the Ephesian elders about had come true: false teachers were in the church (Acts 20:28–30). The pastor's job is to warn them and teach the people the truth. If he abandoned the flock, Timothy would be a hireling and not a shepherd (John 10:12–13).

For the Lord's sake (12–17). Jesus died to save sinners, and

He lives to equip and enable His servants to do the work of the ministry. The same God who empowered Paul could empower Timothy—and can empower us today. God is faithful!

For our own sake (18-20). God had equipped Timothy, called him, and given him a solemn charge. There was a battle to fight, and he dare not run away. If we flee the post of duty, we rob ourselves of opportunities to grow, to serve, and to glorify God.

When the winds of adversity blow, set your sails in the right direction, and let Christ handle the rudder. Otherwise, you may be shipwrecked.

◆

Responsibility   Someone defined responsibility as "our response to God's ability."

1 TIMOTHY 2

What is the most vital ministry of the local church? According to Paul, it is *prayer*. Prayer moves the hand that governs the world. We must pray for government leaders, that the doors of ministry will be kept open and souls will be won to Christ. Because God's people do not pray for people in authority, wars close mission fields, officials do not grant needed visas, and the work of the Lord suffers.

> 66 *A good woman is the best thing on earth. Women were last at the cross and first at the open tomb. The church owes a debt to her faithful women which she can never estimate, to say nothing of the debt we owe in our homes to godly wives and mothers.* 99

Vance Havner

Paul reminds Christian men that Christian women are important to the Lord and to the work of the church. The gospel brought freedom to women in the Roman Empire, but some of them did not know how to handle it and went to extremes asserting their liberty. Hence, the reminder about the spiritual leadership of the men in the church.

Modesty, true spiritual beauty (1 Pet. 3:1–6), godliness, and good works—these will characterize the woman God blesses.

> **❝***It is in willing submission, rather than grudging capitulation, that the woman in the church (whether married or single) and the wife in the home find their fulfillment.***❞**
>
> Elisabeth Elliot

1 TIMOTHY 3

Being a leader of God's people is a serious task, and no one should accept an office who is not qualified and willing to *use* that office to help the church.

Watching (1–7). The title *bishop* means "overseer" and describes the work of the elder (Acts 20:17, 28). God's people are like sheep; they need shepherds to watch over them, protect them, and lead them. Pray for your spiritual leaders that they might more and more be what God wants them to be.

Working (8–13). The word *deacon* means "servant." The deacons assist the elders in carrying out the work of the church (Acts 6:1–7). As with the elders, the deacons should be qualified spiritually and set the right example in their homes.

Worshiping (14–16). The church is much more than a group of like-minded people who assemble from time to time. The living God is in their midst (Matt. 18:20), and the truth of God has been deposited with them! They worship the Son of God who alone is worthy of praise! Yes, it is a serious thing to be a part of a local church. Do you take it seriously?

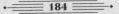

1 TIMOTHY 4

Watch yourself (1–5). Satan is at work spreading false doctrine, and his ministers are already in the church (2 Cor. 11:13–15). God's servants must preach the truth and fight the devil's lies. Declaring war may not make us popular, but it will keep us faithful.

Exercise yourself (6–10). If believers would put as much effort into the spiritual life as they do their recreation and hobbies, what a difference it would make! Physical exercise is important, but spiritual exercise is even more essential. Both discipline and devotion are needed to make a winning athlete and an effective Christian.

Give yourself (11–16). It takes real effort to grow in the Christian life and to be successful in Christian service. God asks for our wholehearted surrender, no matter what the cost. Ponder these admonitions that Paul wrote to Timothy and see how they apply in your life.

Advance!   *The word translated "progress" in 1 Timothy 4:15 means "pioneer advance." As we walk with the Lord and serve Him, we must move into new territory and not stay the same spiritually. There are new truths to learn, new battles to fight, and new victories to win. "Restlessness is discontent," said Thomas Alva Edison, "and discontent is the first necessity of progress. Show me a thoroughly satisfied man and I will show you a failure."*

1 TIMOTHY 5

What causes problems in churches? Often, it is people not getting along with each other. Brothers and sisters do not always dwell together in unity (Ps. 133).

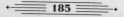

Paul suggests that we treat other people the way we would treat members of our own family (vv. 1–2). If the older people complain about things, deal with them as you would your father or mother, and accept the younger believers as brothers and sisters. This is simply a call to love others as God loves you.

Not everybody who asks for help should receive it (vv. 3–16). Charity should begin at home (vv. 4, 16), and church leaders must exercise discernment lest they create more problems than they solve.

Sometimes trouble comes because we believe reports that cannot be verified (v. 19), or we show partiality (v. 21), or we make decisions before getting the facts (v. 22). Not every church member has a character as good as his or her reputation (vv. 24–25), so take care!

1 TIMOTHY 6

Watch your motives (1–2). Be obedient so you do not bring reproach on the Word (v. 1; Titus 2:10) or show disrespect for persons in authority over you (v. 2). Never take advantage of fellow believers; rather, do all you can to help them.

Watch your attitudes (3–5). Do you enjoy arguing about the Bible? Then search your heart to see if any of these sinful attitudes are hiding there. You can never debate people into the kingdom or into a more sanctified life.

Watch your values (6–10, 17–19). Are you content with the necessities of life, or must God give you luxuries? God wants you to enjoy His gifts (v. 17) and employ them for the good of others; but beware when your heart is set on getting rich (Prov. 15:27; Eccles. 5:10).

Watch your testimony (11–16). Know the things you should flee, follow, and fight, and do not confuse them. When you think it too difficult to stand up for the Lord, remember how He stood up for you.

Watch your stewardship (20–21). You have a deposit of spiritual truth to guard and invest (1:18; 2 Tim. 1:14; 2:2), and the enemy wants to take it from you. Beware those who want to give you "new knowledge" beyond what God says in His Word.

Proper Conduct

First Timothy tells you how to "conduct yourself in the house of God" (3:15). This involves exercising yourself (4:7), giving yourself (4:15), taking heed to yourself (4:16), saving yourself (4:16), keeping yourself pure (5:22), and withdrawing yourself from troublemakers (6:5). Are you taking care of yourself as the Lord directs?

SECOND TIMOTHY

◆

Paul's freedom did not last long. He was arrested again, taken to Rome for trial, and eventually executed. He wrote this letter to his beloved son in the faith to encourage him to remain strong in the Lord (chaps. 1—2), to explain the perilous times (chap. 3), and to urge him to come to Rome as soon as possible (chap. 4). This very personal letter focuses on faithfulness in the ministry.

It was a difficult time for Paul. Not only was he facing trial and almost certain death, but he was abandoned by the believers who should have stood with him (1:15; 4:16). His statement in 4:6–8 is one of the greatest confessions of faith in the Bible.

We are now in those perilous times that Paul wrote about centuries ago. This letter teaches us how to live and serve successfully in them.

2 TIMOTHY 1

Perhaps some of the "enemies" that attacked Timothy are attacking you and making you want to give up.

Self-pity (4). Timothy was having a hard time in Ephesus and wanted to leave (1 Tim. 1:3). Perhaps that caused his tears. When you start feeling sorry for yourself, remember that others are praying for you and that God still honors your faith.

Neglect (6). Timothy had neglected his spiritual life (1 Tim. 4:14), and the flame was low on the altar of his heart. No wonder he needed to exercise himself (1 Tim. 4:7–8)!

Timidity (7). *Fear* in this verse means "cowardice" or "timidity." Timothy was not enthusiastic in his witness or ministry. The Holy Spirit can give us the resources we need to get the job done.

Shame (8, 12, 16). Paul was not ashamed of the gospel (Rom. 1:16) or of the Lord. His friend Onesiphorus was not ashamed of being identified with Paul (v. 16). Timothy should not be ashamed of either the Lord or Paul (v. 8).

Carelessness (13–14). Paul committed the message to Timothy, and Timothy's responsibility was to guard it (1 Tim. 6:20) and share it with others (2 Tim. 2:2). Again, the Spirit of God enables us to be faithful.

2 TIMOTHY 2

God's grace strengthens us and enables us to be faithful teachers (v. 2), soldiers (vv. 3–4), athletes (v. 5), farmers (v. 6), workers (v. 15), vessels (vv. 20–23), and servants (vv. 24–26). The world looks on us as evildoers; but we are God's elect, willing to live and die for Jesus Christ (vv. 8–13).

God's grace enables us to overcome our three great enemies: the world (v. 4), the flesh (v. 22), and the devil (v. 26).

God's grace enables us to endure hardship (vv. 3, 10) as we fight the Lord's battles, so that we do not deny the Lord (vv. 11–13). It helps us do work of which we are not ashamed (v. 15) and deal with problem people of whom we are not afraid (vv. 23–26).

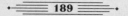*Grace is but glory begun, and glory is but grace perfected.*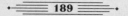

Jonathan Edwards

---

2 TIMOTHY 3

Perilous in verse 1 means "difficult," "hard to deal with," or "dangerous." It is the same Greek word used to describe the demoniac in Matthew 8:28 and translated "exceedingly fierce." How do we live for Christ in such terrible times?

Expect them (1–9). The person who is looking for a soon-coming paradise on earth is destined for disappointment. To expect these perilous times is to become not a pessimist but a realist. Note the emphasis on the wrong kind of love (vv. 2, 4).

Follow the right examples (10–12). We tend to emulate the people we admire, so be careful about the heroes you select. Modern-day Christian celebrities may not exemplify the lifestyle God wants us to have.

Stay with the Bible (13–17). Believe God's Word will save you (v. 15), mature you from childhood to adulthood (vv. 15, 17), and equip you to serve the Lord (v. 17). Satanic deception is rampant today and has infected the church (v. 13), and the only weapon that defeats the deceivers is God's inspired Word.

Watch for Counterfeits!

> Jannes and Jambres (v. 8) were magicians in Pharaoh's court who imitated the miracles that Moses performed (Exod. 7:8–13). Satan is an imitator who produces counterfeit Christians (vv. 5, 13; 2 Cor. 11:13–15) who infiltrate the church and create divisions. God's people need discernment in these difficult days.

---

2 TIMOTHY 4

Christ is coming (1)! In view of this, we must know our task and be faithful to do it. Review 2 Corinthians 5:9–11, and read 1 John 2:28–3:2.

Apostasy is coming (2–5)! Indeed, it is now here. Many professed Christians have no "ear" for the Word of God. They prefer religious entertainment and sermons that will tickle their ears instead of cut their hearts.

Departure is coming (6–8)! Paul saw his approaching death as the offering of a sacrifice to God (v. 6; Phil. 2:17), the ending of a difficult race (v. 7), and the gaining of a glorious crown (v. 8; Rev. 2:10). This is the victor's crown given to winners at the Greek Olympic Games.

Help is coming (9–22)! Paul was greatly disappointed when

the people he had ministered to turned away from him and were ashamed of his bonds. He asked Timothy to come as soon as possible and to bring Mark with him. But best of all, the Lord came to Paul and encouraged him! No matter what His people may do, Jesus will never leave you or forsake you (Acts 18:9–11; Heb. 13:5–6).

Respond to Opportunities

Paul's plea, "Come before winter" (2 Tim. 4:21), is a reminder to us that opportunities do not wait forever. Once the winter season began, Timothy could not travel easily to Rome and see his beloved friend for the last time. "Before winter or never!" said Dr. Clarence Macartney in his famous sermon "Come Before Winter." He continued, "There are some things which will never be done unless they are done 'before winter.'" Are there opportunities you are neglecting today that may soon vanish forever? Are there people you should contact and decisions you should make? Today is yours; tomorrow may be too late. Come before winter!

TITUS

◆

Titus was a Greek (Gal. 2:3) whom Paul won to Christ (Titus 1:4) and enlisted in service. Like Timothy, he became one of Paul's special assistants, sent to the churches to represent the apostle. He was serving in Crete when this letter was written. Paul wrote it, probably from Corinth, after his release from prison.

The letter emphasizes good works (1:16; 2:7, 14; 3:1, 8, 14). We are not saved by good works (3:5), but good works are one evidence of salvation. Apparently the saints on Crete were better at professing the faith than practicing it.

After his greeting (1:1–4), Paul gives the qualifications (1:5–9) and duties (1:10–16) of elders and urges Titus to organize the local churches and deal with the false teachers. He then tells Titus how to minister to various kinds of people in the church (2:1–3:11) and closes the letter with personal information (3:12–14) and a farewell (3:15).

TITUS 1

Titus wanted another assignment from Paul because he was having a hard time ministering in Crete. When you feel like quitting, follow the counsel Paul gave to Titus.

Focus on the privileges of ministry (1–4). God declares His truth through dedicated people, and it is a joy to share the Word with others. The angels in heaven would love to change places with us, so we should never cease to marvel that God would use us!

Obey the Word (5–9). Sometimes there are problems because unqualified people get into places of leadership or because places of leadership have not been filled. The Greek word translated "set in order" is a medical term that means

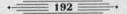

4:4), a living hope (1 Pet. 1:3), a stabilizing hope and a purifying hope (1 John 3:3).

...my work in the morning without thinking ...He may interrupt my work and begin His ...ot looking for death, I am looking for Him.

G. Campbell Morgan

...need frequent reminders!

...ber what you should do (1–2). Christians are citi-...rth as well as citizens of heaven, and they should be ...f people described in these two brief verses.

...ber what you were (3). God has forgotten our sins; ...ould, too; but it does us good to remember what it ...o be a lost sinner. (See Deut. 5:15; 15:15; 24:18, 22; ...4.)

...ber what God did for you (4–7). Did you deserve to ...ospel and receive the gift of eternal life? No, it all ...because of God's kindness, love, and grace. "He ...—we did not save ourselves. He has washed away ...e stand justified in His sight; and we face the future ...w because we are the heirs of God.

...ber what God expects of you (8–11). A major theme ...er is *good works* (1:16; 2:7, 14; 3:1, 8, 14). People who ...r the Lord do not have time for useless arguments.

"to set a broken bone." The
avoid facing and solving ser

Face the enemy (10–16). P
Titus was too timid to confr
done. "Sound doctrine" (v. 9)
ing that contributes to the sp
as a physician must attack
church leaders must attack

A Pure Mind

"To the
1:15) c
tary la
mean t
after be
God's
you wi
avoid t
science
can en

TITUS 2

Living (1–10). Whether w
gle, we are all needed in th
for us to do. One test of spir
cept and minister to a var
blasphemes the Word (v. 5)
who minister should set the

Learning (11–12). God's
teaches us how to live the C
grace as an excuse for sin
power (Rom. 6:1; Jude 4). Th
renews us so that we want

Looking (13–15). What s
The return of Jesus Chri
blessed hope; it is a joyful

---

hope (Ep
(Heb. 6:1

—

“ *I never beg
that perha
own. I am*

—

TITUS

We all
Remer
zens of ea
the kind
Remer
and we s
was like
1 Pet. 4:1

Remer
hear the
happene
saved us
our sins;
confident

Remer
in this let
are busy

PHILEMON

Providen*ce.* While a prisoner in Rome, Paul met Onesimus
("unprofitable" [v. 11]), a runaway slave who belonged to Philemon, a friend Paul had led to Christ (v. 19). Paul won Onesimus
to Christ and sent him back to his master in Colosse (Col. 4:7–
9). The providence of God is amazing, that Paul and Onesimus
should meet in the great city of Rome! Perhaps Philemon's
prayers brought the men together (v. 22). Philemon certainly
saw Romans 8:28 in action!

Friendship. Paul has so much good to say about Philemon.
He was a beloved friend, a man of faith and love, a refreshing
Christian, a praying man, a man who obeyed God's will. Can
your friends say these things about you?

Accepted and Redeemed	*Two statements in Paul's letter to Phile-mon remind us of what Jesus did for us. "Receive him [Onesimus] as you would me" (v. 17) reminds us that we are "ac-cepted in the Beloved" (Eph. 1:6). "Put that on my account" (v. 18) reminds us that Jesus paid the price for our redemp-tion (Rom. 4:1–8; 2 Cor. 5:21).*

Reconciliation. According to Roman law, Onesimus could
have been executed for his crimes. But he had become a
brother in Christ, and Philemon had to forgive him and take

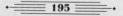

him back. True reconciliation is not cheap; there is a price to pay. Paul knew this and was willing to pay the price himself. Can God use you as a reconciler? Are you willing to pay the price?

"to set a broken bone." The church body suffers when we avoid facing and solving serious problems.

Face the enemy (10–16). Perhaps like Timothy (2 Tim. 1:7), Titus was too timid to confront the enemy; but it had to be done. "Sound doctrine" (v. 9) means "healthy doctrine," teaching that contributes to the spiritual health of the church. Just as a physician must attack infection and disease, so local church leaders must attack false doctrine.

A Pure Mind	*"To the pure all things are pure"* (Titus 1:15) *concerns false teaching about dietary laws* (1 Tim. 4:2–5). *It does not mean that a "pure mind" remains pure after beholding what is impure. When God's truth enlightens your conscience, you will know right from wrong and will avoid that which is evil. A defiled conscience is like a dirty window: no light can enter* (Matt. 6:22–23).

TITUS 2

Living (1–10). Whether we are young or old, married or single, we are all needed in the local church; and God has a job for us to do. One test of spiritual fellowship is its ability to accept and minister to a variety of people. How we live either blasphemes the Word (v. 5) or beautifies it (v. 10), and those who minister should set the example (vv. 7–8).

Learning (11–12). God's grace not only saves us but also teaches us how to live the Christian life. Those who use God's grace as an excuse for sin have never experienced its saving power (Rom. 6:1; Jude 4). The same grace that redeems us also renews us so that we want to obey His Word (v. 14).

Looking (13–15). What starts with grace will lead to glory! The return of Jesus Christ for His people is more than a blessed hope; it is a joyful hope (Rom. 5:2; 12:12), a unifying

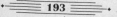

hope (Eph. 4:4), a living hope (1 Pet. 1:3), a stabilizing hope (Heb. 6:19), and a purifying hope (1 John 3:3).

❝_I never begin my work in the morning without thinking that perhaps He may interrupt my work and begin His own. I am not looking for death, I am looking for Him._**❞**

G. Campbell Morgan

TITUS 3

We all need frequent reminders!

Remember what you should do (1–2). Christians are citizens of earth as well as citizens of heaven, and they should be the kind of people described in these two brief verses.

Remember what you were (3). God has forgotten our sins, and we should, too; but it does us good to remember what it was like to be a lost sinner. (See Deut. 5:15; 15:15; 24:18, 22; 1 Pet. 4:1–4.)

Remember what God did for you (4–7). Did you deserve to hear the gospel and receive the gift of eternal life? No, it all happened because of God's kindness, love, and grace. "He saved us"—we did not save ourselves. He has washed away our sins; we stand justified in His sight; and we face the future confidently because we are the heirs of God.

Remember what God expects of you (8–11). A major theme in this letter is _good works_ (1:16; 2:7, 14; 3:1, 8, 14). People who are busy for the Lord do not have time for useless arguments.

HEBREWS

❧

The author of Hebrews is unknown to us, but the theme of the book is clear: "Let us go on to perfection [spiritual maturity]!" (6:1). The epistle was written to Jewish believers who were tempted to abandon the fullness of Christ and go back to the emptiness of a religious system soon to be destroyed.

Lost people are still "in Egypt" and need to be redeemed through faith in Christ. Those who are redeemed are privileged to enter their spiritual inheritance ("Canaan") and enjoy His "rest" (4:11; Matt. 11:28–30). Entering Canaan is not a type of going to heaven. It is a picture of conquering the enemy and claiming your spiritual inheritance by faith.

But too many believers, like Israel in the Old Testament, are wandering in the wilderness of unbelief and yearning to go back to the old life. The message of Hebrews is especially for them: "Let us go on to maturity!"

Hebrews is one of three New Testament letters written to explain Habakkuk 2:4, "The just shall live by his faith." (See Rom. 1:17; Gal. 3:11; Heb. 10:38.) The emphasis in Hebrews is on "by faith." God has spoken through His Son, and we must respond to that Word. Our response determines the kind of life we live and how much of our spiritual inheritance we claim. We are not only *saved* by faith, but we must *live* by faith.

One key word in Hebrews is *better*. Christ is better than the angels (chaps. 1—2) and better than Moses and Aaron (chaps. 3—6). He has a better priesthood (chap. 7), covenant (chap. 8), sanctuary (chap. 9), and sacrifice (chap. 10); and He gives His people a better life (chaps. 11—13), a life of faith.

As you meditate on this profound letter, ask yourself: Am I looking back and craving the old life, or am I pressing on by faith to claim my inheritance in Christ? Am I wandering in a

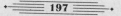

wilderness of unbelief or resting in His finished work and faithful Word?

HEBREWS 1

"God has spoken to us!" What a tremendous statement, and what a great responsibility it brings to you if you have heard His voice through His Word: "See that you do not refuse Him who speaks" (12:25). What you do with the Word of God determines what you will enjoy of God's will and claim of your inheritance.

Angels

Jesus is greater than the angels because He is the eternal Son of God Whom the angels worship and serve. Angels serve God's people (Heb. 1:14), even though we may not recognize them (Heb. 13:2; Gen. 18). Angels give special care to children (Matt. 18:10) and intervene in the lives of God's servants when they need special help (Acts 5:17–21; 12:1–10). When believers die, the angels escort them to glory (Luke 16:22); and when Christ returns, angels will accompany Him (Matt. 25:31). We must not worship angels (Rev. 22:9) or pray to them; but we can trust God to send them when we need them most.

Jesus Christ is the Father's last word. In Him, divine revelation is *seen* and *heard* in its fullness; and in Him, God's revelation is complete. When we see Him, we see the Father (John 14:1–11). Through Christ, we understand where everything came from, where it is going, what keeps it going, and why it is here.

We also understand what He has done for us. *He died for us!* Today He is enthroned in glory, ministering to us and for us (13:20–21). He wants to mature us and teach us how to walk by faith. One day He will defeat all His enemies and bring in His righteous kingdom.

With a Savior like that, why look for a substitute?

"Other men had the threads of truth; but Christ took the threads, and wove them into a glorious robe, put it on, and came forth clothed with every truth of God."

Charles Haddon Spurgeon

HEBREWS 2

Hear Him (1–4). This is the first of five solemn admonitions to believers to pay attention to what God says in His Word. During Old Testament times, God dealt with those who disobeyed His Word. In these last days, we have a greater obligation to obey because we have the complete Scriptures and the full revelation of God in Jesus Christ. Are you serious about what God says to you?

Secure in the Promise

Ponder these verses: "We wish to see Jesus" (John 12:21), "We see Jesus" (Heb. 2:9), and "We shall see Him [Jesus]" (1 John 3:2). The first is the plea of the sinner; the second is the privilege of the saint; the third is the promise of the Scripture.

See Him (5–9). There is a "world to come," and how you live today will help to determine your place in the future kingdom of Christ (1:13; 10:13; 12:28). Today, we see man fallen in Adam; but by faith, we see Christ and His victory. Because He is glorified, we shall be glorified in Him!

Trust Him (10–18). Persons who trust Christ are God's children (v. 13) on their way to glory (v. 10). The Redeemer has defeated death and the devil, and He understands how His people feel as they face the temptations and trials of life. When you come to Him by faith, you come to a sympathetic High Priest who can meet your every need. Trust Him!

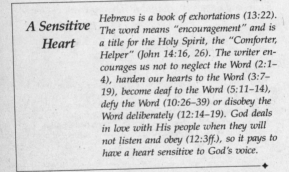

A Sensitive Heart

Hebrews is a book of exhortations (13:22). The word means "encouragement" and is a title for the Holy Spirit, the "Comforter, Helper" (John 14:16, 26). The writer encourages us not to neglect the Word (2:1–4), harden our hearts to the Word (3:7–19), become deaf to the Word (5:11–14), defy the Word (10:26–39) or disobey the Word deliberately (12:14–19). God deals in love with His people when they will not listen and obey (12:3ff.), so it pays to have a heart sensitive to God's voice.

HEBREWS 3

Consider Him (1–6). Hebrews focuses on Jesus Christ. The writer wants us to "see" Him (2:9), "consider" Him (3:1), and keep our eyes of faith fixed on Him (12:1–2). Whenever you are tempted to look at your circumstances or at yourself, look to Jesus by faith and rejoice in His faithfulness.

Obey Him (7–15). The writer uses the failure of Israel as a warning against a hard heart. How does a believer's heart become hard? By refusing His words, despising His works, and being ignorant of His ways. Sin is deceitful. You think you are

getting away with it, but all the while it is hardening your heart and robbing you of blessing.

Believe Him (16–19). Here is another exhortation to faith. The fact that the Jews were delivered from Egypt was no guarantee they would claim their inheritance. Because of their unbelief, they failed to enter the land (Num. 13). An "evil heart of unbelief" (v. 12) will rob you of what God has planned for you in your Christian life, so pay attention to God's Word. As Paul wrote, "Faith comes by hearing, and hearing by the word of God" (Rom. 10:17).

Are You Hearing?

People with hard hearts know the truth but resist it and refuse to obey it. They know that God chastens disobedient children, but they almost defy God to act. They think they can sin and get away with it. The first step toward a hard heart is neglect of the Word of God (Heb. 2:1–4), not taking it seriously. It is either "hearing" or "hardening." Take your choice (Ps. 95).

HEBREWS 4

His rest (1–10). Three different "rests" are in view: God's Sabbath rest after creation (v. 4; Gen. 2:2); Israel's rest of victory in Canaan (v. 3; Josh. 21:44); and the believer's rest of faith today (vv. 1, 9–10). Israel was delivered from Egypt, but a whole generation failed to enter Canaan and claim their promised inheritance. Why? Because of their unbelief. "Let us fear!" (v. 1).

His sight (11–13). God sees the heart and uses His sword to help us see our true spiritual condition (Jer. 17:9). Spend time daily reading the Word and meditating on it, always applying its truths to your heart. One day you will give account to God of what you have done with His Word, so be faithful.

His throne (14–16). You cannot claim your inheritance in your own power or wisdom. But you have a great High Priest who can give you the mercy and the grace you need just when you need them. He lives to intercede for you (7:25) and to help you do His will (13:20–21).

A Throne of Grace	*To the unsaved, God's throne is a throne of judgment (Rev. 20:11–15); but to God's children, it is a throne of grace. When you are tempted, you can come to your great High Priest for mercy and grace. If you sin, you can come to your Advocate for forgiveness (1 John 1:9— 2:2). The way is always open.*

HEBREWS 5

Selected (1–6). Just as the Jewish high priest was appointed by God, so our great High Priest was appointed by the Father (Ps. 110:4); and He alone is worthy to serve. Never allow anybody to come between you and God, for Christ is the only mediator (1 Tim. 2:5). "The order of Melchizedek" refers to Genesis 14:18–24. Being from the tribe of Judah, Jesus could not serve as priest on earth; but He can serve as priest in heaven. He is there ministering for you today.

Perfected (7–10). Jesus had to prepare for His priestly ministry by experiencing the trials His people experience as they walk by faith (4:15). Because of the life that He lived and the death that He died, He is able to identify with your needs and give you grace to see you through. He understands!

Neglected (11–14). The "milk" of the Word represents the "first principles" of the Christian life, that is, what Jesus Christ did for us when He was on earth. The "meat" of the Word is the teaching about what Jesus is now doing for us in heaven, His ministry as High Priest. How sad it is when Christians neglect God's Word and stop growing in grace.

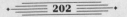

> **Mature in Christ**
>
> *Mature believers understand the heavenly priesthood of Jesus Christ and know how to come to the throne of grace for help. They are skillful in using God's truth in their personal lives, and they can also teach others. Do you qualify?*

HEBREWS 6

The impossible (1–8). The ABC's of the Christian life are important, but they must be a launching pad and not a parking lot, for the challenge is, "Let us go on to maturity." If we get sluggish (v. 12) and dull (5:11) toward the Word, we may fall by the wayside (v. 6; Gal. 6:1) and stop being fruitful. As long as disobedient believers are bringing shame to Christ, it is impossible to bring them to repentance, and God must deal with them.

The improbable (9–12). But the writer did not believe that his readers were in that condition. Although they had a long way to go in their Christian experience, the fruit was there. Diligence, faith, and patience are required to live the Christian life. Maturity is not automatic.

The immutable (13–20). The chapter ends with one of the greatest statements on security found anywhere in Scripture. God's promise and God's oath assure us that we are His, and God's character backs up His words. Instead of drifting (2:1), we are anchored heavenward where Jesus ministers in the very presence of God, and that anchor will not fail. We are anchored so we can make progress!

HEBREWS 7

With this chapter, the writer begins to explain the better priesthood of Christ; and he begins with the *better order,* the order of Melchizedek (Gen. 14).

Jesus Christ is both King and Priest, and His throne is a throne of grace (4:16). As King, He can control circumstances

around you; as Priest, He can change attitudes within you. You will experience righteousness and peace as you yield to Him (v. 2; Pss. 72:7; 85:9–10; Isa. 32:17).

Because He is a Priest forever, He saves forever (vv. 23–25). "To the uttermost" means "completely," "perfectly." You are secure as long as He lives, and He lives eternally. You can live by the power of His endless life!

A perfect salvation should lead to a life of growing maturity. An earthly priesthood can make nothing perfect (v. 11), nor can the law of God (v. 19) or the sacrifices (10:1–2); but Jesus can lead you into spiritual maturity as you walk by faith (13:20–21). He invites you to come to His throne, and He understands you better than you understand yourself.

HEBREWS 8

Finality (1). There were no chairs in the Jewish tabernacle or temple because the priests' work was never finished. But Jesus finished the work of redemption (John 19:30) and sat down on the throne (10:11–14). Rejoice!

Reality (2–6). The Jewish priests in the temple ministered with copies and shadows, but Christ in heaven ministers in the original sanctuary from which the things on earth were copied. When you trust Christ, you enter a life of reality, and you are forever finished with substitutes. Rejoice!

Maturity (7–13). The law of Moses was given to the children of Israel as a tutor to help them grow up and be prepared for their Messiah's coming (Gal. 4:1–7). They were like children; God had to take them by the hand and lead them. But the new covenant, with its heavenly priesthood, leads us to spiritual maturity: God puts His Word in our hearts and transforms our character (2 Cor. 3:1–3, 18).

Rejoice and be exceedingly glad!

HEBREWS 9

A better sanctuary (1–10). In every way, the present heavenly sanctuary is better than any sanctuary on earth, including the temple in Jerusalem. In the earthly temple, the furnishings were only symbols, the work was never finished, and the ministry could never change the human heart. We should

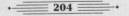

be grateful for the price Jesus paid to make His heavenly ministry possible.

*A **better service*** (11–15). The Jewish high priest could deal only with externals, but Jesus deals with the heart and conscience. He can purify us and perfect us (13:20–21) so that we can serve God acceptably. Do you come to Him daily and ask for His ministry?

*A **better sacrifice*** (16–28). The blood that purchased your eternal redemption came not from unwilling animals but from the Son of God who willingly laid down His life for you (John 10:14–18). The spotless Lamb of God had to die only once; the sacrifice need not be repeated. Have you trusted that blood to save you?

Jesus' Appearings	*Hebrews 9:24–28 mentions three "appearings" of Jesus Christ: a past appearing (v. 26) for our salvation, a present appearing (v. 24) for our sanctification, and a future appearing for our glorification (v. 28).*

HEBREWS 10

Forgiveness (1–18). The sacrifices under the Old covenant brought a *reminder* of sin, not a *remission* of sin. The blood of God's Son took care of sin once and for all. Because there is no more offering for sin, there is also no more remembrance of sin (v. 17; Jer. 31:34), and we can rejoice that we have a righteous standing before God.

Faithfulness (19–25). The same Savior who died for you now lives for you and invites you to come into His presence to worship and to share your needs. The Old Testament high priest could go behind the veil only once a year, but we can come into God's presence any time. Be sure that you are cleansed and prepared to meet Him. You can trust Him: "He who promised is faithful" (v. 23).

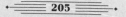

Fearfulness (26–39). The privilege of entering His presence brings with it the responsibility of obeying His precepts. This exhortation applies to those who repeatedly defy God's will and disgrace God's name. God deals with His children; He will not have them acting like rebels. The chapter closes on a note of encouragement. God warns us so that we will not be presumptuous, but He comforts us so that we will not be discouraged. The hard heart needs the warning; the broken heart needs the comfort.

HEBREWS 11

Faith is confidence in God that leads to obedience to God. True faith is based on what God says and is demonstrated in what we do. People with faith *do* things for God, and God does things for them.

Faith is not a luxury; it is a necessity. It is for common people and not just great leaders. We need faith for worshiping (v. 4) as well as for working (v. 7), walking (vv. 8–9), waiting (vv. 10–12), and warring (vv. 30–34). In any area of life where you ignore faith, you will sin (Rom. 14:23).

Steady in the Faith

The great theologian John Calvin defined faith as "a steady and certain knowledge of the Divine benevolence towards us, which, being founded on the truth of the gratuitous promise in Christ, is both revealed to our minds, and confirmed to our hearts, by the Holy Spirit." Note that faith is founded on divine truth (God's promise) and is witnessed to by the Spirit in the heart. It has both objective and subjective aspects, and both are essential.

The phrase "still others" (v. 36) reminds us that we can live by faith and appear to be defeated. Not everybody who

trusted God was delivered or protected (vv. 36–40). But the important thing is not God's deliverance; it is God's approval (v. 39). Faith in God gives you the ability to endure when others are giving up.

Where does this faith come from? Read Romans 10:17 and 15:4.

> ❝Faith makes all things possible;
> love makes all things easy.❞
>
> D. L. Moody

HEBREWS 12

Runners (1–4). The people listed in chapter 11 are the "cloud" that witnesses to us, "God can be trusted! Put your faith in His Word and keep running the race!" When you read the Old Testament, your faith should grow, for the account shows what God did in and through people who dared to trust His promises (Rom. 15:4). When you read the Gospels, you see the greatest example of endurance in Jesus Christ.

> ❝You can judge the quality of their faith from the way
> they behave. Discipline is an index to doctrine.❞
>
> Tertullian

Children (5–11). "Chastening" refers to child training, helping the child prepare for adulthood. It does not necessarily mean punishment for disobedience, although that sometimes might be included. The successful runner must exercise discipline and submit to training. Never fear the chastening hand of the Lord; it is controlled by a loving heart. God's goal is your maturity.

Citizens (12–29). The people of Israel had a frightening ex-

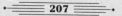

perience of law at Sinai (Exod. 19), but our experience at Mount Zion is one of grace and glory. We are citizens of the heavenly city and will one day fellowship with patriarchs and angels—and God! But this does not mean we can ignore His solemn voice to us. If God is shaking things in your life, listen to His Word. You will discover the things that cannot be shaken, and you will run the race to the end.

"We cry too often to be delivered from the punishment, instead of the sin that lies behind it. We are anxious to escape from the things that cause us pain rather than from the things that cause God pain."

G. Campbell Morgan

HEBREWS 13

Lest we get the idea that we can run the race successfully alone, the writer closes his letter by reminding us to follow our spiritual leaders. If we do, we will love the brothers and sisters (v. 1), help strangers (v. 2) and prisoners (v. 3), live above lust (v. 4) and covetousness (vv. 5–6), and not be led astray by false doctrines (v. 9).

Remember them (7–8). This may refer to leaders now dead, but their ministry goes on. Remember what they taught you, how they lived, and what they lived for. Church leaders may come and go, but Jesus is the same; and they must fix our eyes on Him.

Obey them (17). If they are faithful to care for your soul and teach you the Word, you have the responsibility to obey. A spiritual leader is not a dictator who drives you from behind. He is a shepherd who goes before and leads the way.

Pray for them (18–19). When you come to the throne of grace, ask God to make His shepherds faithful and fruitful.

Pray that the Great Shepherd will use them to "make you complete in every good work" (vv. 20–21).

Greet them (24). You should know your leaders personally and be on good terms with them. Let nothing come between you that could create problems in the fellowship (12:14–15).

JAMES

◆

The man who wrote this letter was the half brother of our Lord (Mark 6:3) and the leader of the church in Jerusalem (Acts 1:14; 12:17; 1 Cor. 15:7). He was a devout Jew and wrote to Jewish believers scattered throughout the Roman world. They were troubled by trials and testings as well as by problems in their assemblies; and James wrote to help them mature in their faith (1:4; 2:22; 3:2).

The epistle of James is a practical book that discusses living the faith. It contains echoes of the Sermon on the Mount and the book of Proverbs, both of which are practical.

If we truly practice our faith, it will be seen in how we face trials (chap. 1), in the way we treat people (chap. 2), in what we say (chap. 3), in how we deal with sin in our lives (chap. 4), and in our prayer life (chap. 5).

JAMES 1

Note some essentials for mature living.

The wisdom of God (1–11). You need wisdom in your suffering so you will not waste your suffering and miss the spiritual growth that should result. When you trust God, trials work for you and not against you; but be sure your heart is wholly yielded to Him. If your heart and mind are divided, trials will tear you apart.

The goodness of God (12–20). When you realize how good God is to you, you will have no interest in the temptations the enemy puts before you. When you are tempted, count your blessings; and you will soon have strength to say no.

The Word of God (21–27). The Word gives us spiritual birth (v. 18; 1 Pet. 1:22–23). It is like seed planted in the heart that produces spiritual fruit (v. 21). It is a mirror that helps us ex-

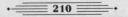

amine ourselves (vv. 23–25) and cleanse our lives. We must *do* the Word of God, not just read it or study it; the blessing is in the *doing*.

❝ *He is already half false who speculates on truth and does not do it. Truth is given, not to be contemplated, but to be done.* **❞**

F. W. Robertson

Word Pictures	*In his letter, James relies on many illustrations from nature. In chapter 1, he compares doubt to the waves of the sea (v. 6), riches to fading flowers (vv. 9–10), and sin to pregnancy (vv. 13–15; Ps. 7:14), weeds (v. 21), and dirt (v. 27). As you continue to read, notice how James uses pictures to make truth vivid and memorable.*

JAMES 2

If you have true saving faith, you will practice *impartiality* (vv. 1–13) and see people in terms of character and not clothing. You will not cater to the rich or ignore the poor, but you will love each person for the sake of Jesus Christ. Christian love simply means treating others the way the Lord treats you and doing it in the power of the Spirit.

True saving faith is also seen in *activity* (vv. 14–26). Faith is not something you only talk about; it is something that motivates your life so that you think of others and serve them. Abraham was saved by faith (Gen. 15:6), but he proved that

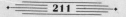

faith by obeying God and offering his son (Gen. 22). Rahab was saved by trusting God (Heb. 11:31), but she showed the reality of her faith by protecting the spies (Josh. 2; 6:17-27).

James and Paul do not contradict each other (Rom. 4:1-5; 5:1); they complement each other. We are justified (declared righteous) before God by faith, but we are justified before men by works. God can see our faith, but men can see only our works.

JAMES 3

The believers James wrote to were having problems with their tongues (1:26; 2:12; 4:1, 11-12). Of course, the tongue is not the problem; it is the *heart* (v. 14; Matt. 12:35-37). But before you say anything, ask yourself some questions.

Who is in control (1-4)? If your tongue is under God's control, you will take what you say seriously (v. 1), and your whole body will be under His discipline (v. 2). Just as a horse needs a rider holding the reins, and a ship needs a pilot at the rudder, so your tongue needs a master; and God is the only one who can do the job. Psalm 141:1-4 is a good prayer if you need help in this area.

❝ *Of your unspoken words, you are the master; of your spoken words, the servant; of your written words, the slave.* **❞**

Quaker Proverb

What will the consequences be (5-12)? Are you starting a fire that may get out of control and do a lot of damage? Are you turning loose a dangerous beast or poisoning a refreshing spring? Once your words are spoken, you cannot take them back, so look ahead.

What are my motives (13-18)? Is there bitterness in your heart or envy? Are you speaking from God's wisdom or the wisdom of the world? Are you a peacemaker or a troublemaker? If your heart is right before God (Heb. 4:12), He will use your words to produce the right kind of fruit.

JAMES 4

Of the early church, it was said, "Behold how they love one another!" Today, people might say, "Behold how they compete with one another!" Why is it sometimes so difficult for God's people to get along?

Selfishness (1–3). The wars among us are caused by the wars within us. We want to please ourselves, even if it hurts somebody else. If we are not careful, even our prayers can become selfish!

Worldliness (4). Because Abraham was separated from sin, he was the friend of God (2:23); but Lot was the friend of the world (Gen. 13:1–13). Ponder 1 John 2:15–17.

Pride (5–10). Satan knows how to use pride to defeat you as he defeated Eve (Gen. 3:1–6). Are you laughing when you should be weeping over your sins? Are you resisting the devil or resisting the Lord?

"It is right for the church to be in the world; it is wrong for the world to be in the church. A boat in water is good; that is what boats are for. However, water inside the boat causes it to sink.**"**

Harold Lindsell

"A whole new generation of Christians has come up believing that it is possible to 'accept' Christ without forsaking the world.**"**

A. W. Tozer

Criticism (11–12). One of the easiest ways to hide our sins is to expose the sins of others. Gossip and slander grieve the Spirit and divide the family. God called us to be witnesses, not judges!

Boasting (13–17). Life is short and the future unknown, so do the will of God today. When you make plans, always say, "If the Lord wills" (Prov. 27:1).

JAMES 5

In these last days, before the coming of the Lord, what does God want in our lives?

Priorities (1–6). To live only to get wealth is to rob yourself of true riches (1 Tim. 6:6–10, 17–19). It is to worry instead of worship (Matt. 6:19–34). God knows you have needs, and He will meet them if you practice Matthew 6:33.

Patience (7–12). If you have sown the right seed, you will eventually reap a harvest of blessing, so be patient. If others have exploited you, be patient; the Judge is at the door. If you are going through trials, be patient; God is still on the throne.

Prayer (13–18). Many kinds of prayer are named here: prayer for the sick, prayer for forgiveness, prayer for the nation, even prayer about the weather. There is no need that prayer cannot meet and no problem that prayer cannot solve.

Personal concern (19–20). Once again, James emphasizes ministry to individuals (1:27; 2:1–4, 14–16). Can you detect when a fellow believer starts to stray? Are you truly concerned? Will you try to help? Will you wait too long?

FIRST PETER

◆

The apostle Peter was chosen to be the first to take the gospel to the Gentiles (Acts 10; 15:7), but his ministry was primarily to the Jews (Gal. 2:1–10). He wrote these two letters to believers scattered in five areas of the Roman Empire, two of which Paul had not been allowed to enter (Acts 16:7). In writing these letters, Peter fulfilled the commission given him in Luke 22:32 and John 21:15–17.

The theme of the first letter is *the grace of God* (5:12), and Peter tells us how to live as aliens in a hostile world. The theme of the second letter is *spiritual knowledge* (he uses *knowledge* seven times in the letter), and he warns us about false teachers.

Peter opens his first epistle by reminding his readers of what God's grace has done for them in saving them (1:1–2:10). He then points out that God's grace helps them in various relationships of life (2:11–3:12) and in the coming time of persecution (3:13–5:14). Peter sums up the themes of both letters in his benediction in 2 Peter 3:18: "But grow in the grace [1 Pet.] and knowledge [2 Pet.] of our Lord and Savior Jesus Christ." That is the only way to succeed in these last days.

1 PETER 1

Salvation is a calling (1–2, 15). We are chosen by the Father, who gives us the new birth (v. 3). We are set apart by the Spirit, who gave the Word and enables God's servants to declare it (vv. 10–12), and gives sinners the faith to believe the promise (v. 22). We have been purchased by the blood of God's Son (vv. 18–21), who died for us, rose again, and is coming for us to give us our inheritance (vv. 3–4, 13). No wonder Peter opened his letter with a song of praise! (See Eph. 1:3–14.)

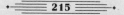

Salvation is a birth (3, 23). This is the spiritual birth Jesus tried to explain to Nicodemus (John 3). When you put your *faith* in Jesus Christ (vv. 5, 7, 9, 21), you are born from above. You receive *hope* (vv. 3–4, 13, 21) and *love* for Christ (v. 8) and His people (v. 22). Because we are God's children, we want to obey Him (vv. 14–16).

Salvation is a redemption (17–21). The apostle is referring to the Passover Feast (Exod. 12). Jesus is the Lamb slain for us, and His blood was sprinkled to shelter us (v. 2). The Jews in Egypt had to be ready to depart, and we must have the same attitude (v. 13). When Jesus comes again, we will make our exodus from this world!

And all of this was "for you" (vv. 4, 10, 12, 13, 20, 25). Are you praising Him?

| *Living Hope* | Men's hopes are dead hopes. Like cut flowers, they bloom awhile and then fade and die (1 Pet. 1:24–25). The Christian's hope is fresh and fruitful because it is a "living hope" (v. 3), purchased by the living Christ (v. 3) and promised in the living Word (v. 23). |

---

1 PETER 2

Growing (1–3). Just as a baby has an appetite for the mother's milk, so the child of God has an appetite for the Father's Word. If you lose that appetite and stop growing, check to see if any of the sins listed in verse 1 are infecting your life.

Building (4–8). God is building a temple out of living stones (Eph. 2:19–22), and we are privileged to be part of it. We are built on Jesus Christ, so there is no way the temple can be destroyed.

Sacrificing (9–10). Each believer is a priest before God and can bring sacrifices to the Lord through Jesus Christ. As we

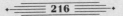

worship the Lord, we proclaim His virtues to a lost world. That is what God called Israel to do (Exod. 19:1–9), and they failed. Are we also failing?

Abstaining (11–12). As strangers whose citizenship is in heaven, we are carefully watched by the world; and we must live to glorify God. It may be difficult today, but it will be worth it when Jesus returns.

Submitting (13–25). Peter's counsel is that Christians be good citizens and employees so that God will be glorified. (See Jeremiah's advice to the captives [Jer. 29].) The example for us to follow is Jesus Christ who submitted even to death.

1 PETER 3

Peter compared believers to sheep (2:25), and sheep are gentle animals. He then called for Christians to practice gentleness in several areas of life.

In the home (1–7). Christian wives with unsaved husbands should seek to win them to the Lord with true spiritual beauty and not with artificial glamour or nagging. External glamour may fade, but a meek and quiet spirit is incorruptible. Husbands should live as though their wives were priceless porcelain vases and treat them with gentle love.

In the church (8–12). Imagine having to remind Christians to show one another love and courtesy! But as James 4 shows, not every local assembly is a place of peace.

In the world (13–22). Anybody can suffer for doing wrong, but Christians must learn to suffer for doing what is right. Of course, Jesus is the example for us to follow (v. 18; 2:18–25). We witness not by making noise and fighting back but by showing meekness and fear (v. 15). A gentle witness can make a big difference in a violent world.

"*Nothing is so strong as gentleness, and nothing so gentle as real strength.***"**

Francis de Sales

A Godly Life

The Christians who received Peter's letter were being slandered by others (2:12, 15, 23; 3:9, 16; 4:4, 14). Peter told them that the best weapon against slander was a godly life that nobody could criticize. H. A. Ironside said, "If what they say about you is true, mend your ways. If it isn't true, forget it, and go on and serve the Lord."

1 PETER 4

Do not be controlled by the past (1–6). People who have been born again through faith in Christ (1:23) should not allow the old life to control them. The past has been buried, and they are new creatures in Christ. Furthermore, life is too short to waste it on godless living, especially when you realize that one day we will all stand before God.

Persecution

Peter said that judgment begins at the house (church) of God (1 Pet. 4:17). The first purpose of persecution is to purify the church so that it will be able to witness to the lost. But it is also a warning to the lost. If God judges His own children for their sins, how much more will He judge lost sinners! (See Prov. 11:31; Ezek. 9.)

Be serious about the present (7–11). No matter how difficult life may be, there is a job to do; and we must be faithful. Take time to pray. Show love to the saints. Use your gifts and tal-

ents to serve others. The Lord who gave you the
also give you the strength to use it for His glory.

Be prepared for the future (12–19). A "fiery trial"
to come to the church. Peter told his readers to expe
as an opportunity to witness for Christ, and in all th
to glorify God. The trial came under the Roman empe
who accused the Christians of burning Rome. The ch
day faces persecution. Are you prepared?

1 PETER 5

Even apart from the end-times suffering that the c
will experience, believers must face their three great ene

The world (1–4). Christian leaders are tempted to ac
the world and "lord it over" God's people (Matt. 20:20–28)
leaders are shepherds, and sheep must be *led,* not *driven.*
service must be willing and humble; we must be eager to h
others.

The flesh (5–7). By nature, we do not want to submit
others. The phrase "clothed with humility" reminds us of ou
Savior when He wore a towel and washed Peter's feet (Joh
13:1–11). If we are submitted to the Lord, we will submit to Hi
people. Humility leads to honor; pride leads to shame.

The devil (8–14). The devil is an adversary, not a friend; he
is a roaring lion, not a playful pet. He wants to devour you, and
you had better be on guard. Peter thought he was well able to
defeat the enemy, so he did not heed the Lord's warning (Luke
22:31–34). The results were failure and shame. You can resist
Satan by faith if you are wearing the armor and trusting the
Spirit (Eph. 6:10–20).

D PETER

, the apostle was conscious that death
that the church was in danger, for false
ng in. He urged the believers to hold to
and grow spiritually (chap. 1), to identify
hers (chap. 2), and to keep the promise of
ppermost in their hearts (chap. 3). He
knowledge that comes from God's Word.

the present (1–11). When you trusted Christ, He
that you need for life and godliness. All you have
appropriate what you need from His resources. His
is the divine nature within, and you can grow in
ge and in grace. This is not automatic; you must be
to use the means of grace that God has provided.

urance from the past (12–18). Peter would be martyred
John 21:18), so he took occasion to remind his readers
hey could trust the Word of God. Although Peter's experi-
e on the Mount of Transfiguration was wonderful (Matt.
1–13), experiences are not a substitute for the unchanging
ord of God.

Hope for the future (19–21). The Word is a light in this dark
world, pointing to the return of the Lord. "Private interpretation" means that no prophecy should be isolated from the rest
of Scripture or interpreted apart from the leading of the Spirit
who gave it to us. The Spirit wrote one Book, and it must be
understood as a whole. Believers may differ on individual matters of prophecy, but they all agree on the "one hope" (Eph.
4:4)—Jesus is coming again!

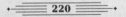

2 PETER 2

The description of the false teachers is clear enough to help you detect them and vivid enough to make you want to avoid them. It is not enough to reject their false teachings. You must also reject their way of life and the hypocrisy behind it.

Their tool is deception, so you must know God's Word and exercise discernment when you hear their impressive language (v. 18) and alluring promises (v. 19). They fellowship with you only to find out what they can get from you (vv. 12–14), and then they will leave you in worse shape than they found you. They are deceptive and destructive, so beware!

Their purpose is personal pleasure and financial gain, and their destiny is judgment. Like Balaam (Num. 22—24), they cause others to sin by using religion for personal gain. They are not God's sheep; they are pigs and dogs in sheep's clothing (Prov. 26:11; Matt. 7:15) and eventually go back to their natural habits. True sheep keep themselves clean because they follow the Shepherd (John 10:27–28).

2 PETER 3

When false teachers cannot accomplish their devious purposes with lies, they start to scoff and ridicule the Word of God. They want you to forget that the very Word they deride is in control of God's universe. God created everything by His Word, and His Word holds it together (Col. 1:16–17; Heb. 1:1–2). His Word caused the Flood (Gen. 6—9), and His Word will one day bring a judgment of fire to the ungodly world (vv. 7–10).

"The Dreadful Day"

"The darkness grows thicker around us, and godly servants of the Most High become rarer and more rare. Impiety and licentiousness are rampant throughout the world, and we live like pigs, like wild beasts, devoid of all reason. But a voice will soon be heard thundering forth: 'Be-

> *hold, the bridegroom cometh!' God will
> not be able to bear this wicked world
> much longer, but will come, with the
> dreadful day, and chastise the scorners of
> his Word." Does that sound like a state-
> ment by one of our contemporary pro-
> phetic preachers? It was said by Martin
> Luther, who lived from 1483 to 1546. If
> Luther felt that the Lord's return was
> near in his day, what should we think
> today!*

Whoever robs you of God's Word robs you of your future.
People who have no future hope have no motivation for life
today. No wonder Peter closes with "Beloved, be diligent!"
(v. 14) and "Beloved, beware!" (v. 17). We live in dangerous
days, but the opportunities have never been greater. God is
patiently waiting for the lost to trust Christ (v. 15), but he needs
you to share the gospel with them.

FIRST JOHN

The apostle wrote this letter to his dear "little children" (the phrase is used nine times) to help them find assurance of personal salvation (5:13). When you are sure of your salvation, you can have fellowship with God and God's people (1:3), experience joy (1:4), and have victory over sin (2:1–2). John also wrote to warn believers about false teachers (2:26–27; 4:1–6). Both Peter and John were concerned about purity of doctrine in the church; and we should be, too.

Chapters 1–2 focus on *fellowship* and contrast *saying* and *doing*. It is easy to talk the Christian life, but God wants the walk. John emphasizes *sonship* in chapters 3–5 (the phrase "born of God" is used several times) and gives three marks of the true child of God: doing God's will (chap. 3), loving the brethren (chap. 4), and believing the truth (chap. 5).

"God is light" (1:5), and His children should walk in the light. "God is love" (4:8, 16), and His children should walk in love. "The Spirit is truth" (5:6), and God's children should believe and obey the truth.

1 JOHN 1

God wants you to have a *living fellowship* (vv. 1–3) with Him and His children. In Jesus Christ, He has revealed what true life really is. Even though you cannot see Him and touch Him as the apostles did centuries ago, He can still be real to you as His Holy Spirit opens the Word to your heart.

He wants you to have a *joyful fellowship* (v. 4). It is not the fellowship of a slave with a master but that of a child with a parent. God delights in His children (Ps. 18:19) and longs to share His love with them (John 14:19–24). When you are happy in the will of God, you are ready to live for Him and serve Him.

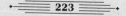

He wants you to have an *honest fellowship* (vv. 5–10). This means "walking in the light" and dealing honestly with sin. Salvation is a matter of life or death, but fellowship is a matter of light or darkness. If you lie to God, to others, and to yourselves, you will lose your fellowship with God and your character. A godly character does not develop in the darkness.

❝Some Christians try to go to heaven alone, in solitude. But believers are not compared to bears or lions or other animals that wander alone. Those who belong to Christ are sheep in this respect, that they love to get together. Sheep go in flocks, and so do God's people.**❞**

Charles Haddon Spurgeon

His Life Was Manifested

Manifest is one of John's favorite words. Jesus was manifested that He might reveal God's life (1 John 1:2), take away our sins (3:5), destroy the devil's works (3:8), and disclose God's love for sinners (4:9).

1 JOHN 2

In Jesus Christ, you have *an Advocate* (vv. 1–2), representing you before God's throne (Zech. 3). When you sin, confess it to Him, and receive His faithful forgiveness.

In Him, you also have *an example* (vv. 3–6), and you should "walk just as He walked." Ask the indwelling Holy Spirit to make you more like Jesus Christ, and saturate yourself with His life as you read the Gospels.

From Jesus Christ, you have *a commandment* (vv. 7–11) to love God's people. The Father gave this commandment to Is-

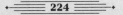

rael (Lev. 19:18) and the Son to His disciples (John 13:34), and the Spirit enables us to obey it (Rom. 5:5).

Because of Jesus Christ, you have *a family* (vv. 12–14). The members are at different stages of spiritual development, but all can receive the Word and grow. How wonderful it is when the "little children" become young men and then fathers!

You also have *some enemies* (vv. 15–27), the world and the false teachers. Christians who love the world lose the enjoyment of the Father's love and the desire to do His will. We overcome the world with God's love and the liars with God's truth (vv. 24–27).

You have *a wonderful hope* (vv. 28–29), the coming of Jesus Christ. Abide in Him so you will not be ashamed when He comes.

1 JOHN 3

Deliberate sin is a serious thing. When you deliberately sin, you grieve the heart of the Father who loves you and has a wonderful future planned for you (vv. 1–3). You grieve the Savior who died for you and delivered you from the power of Satan (vv. 4–8).

Deliberate sin grieves the Holy Spirit who lives in you and gave you new birth (vv. 9–15). You have a new nature and a new Father; therefore, you should live a new life. To John, lack of love is the same as hatred; and hatred is the moral equivalent of murder (Matt. 5:21–26).

Deliberate sin also grieves God's people (vv. 16–24) because we cannot minister to them as we should if we are not walking in love and in the light. Strive to have a heart that is right before God and men (Acts 24:16). Ask God to use you to be an encouragement and help to others (James 2). Love is more than a matter of words (v. 18).

1 JOHN 4

Love is evidence of salvation. If you are born of God through faith in Jesus Christ, you have His nature within (2 Pet. 1:4). Since "God is love" (vv. 8, 16), His children who have His nature should also manifest His love. The children should be like the Father!

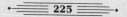

Our love for others makes God's love real and visible to them (v. 12) so we can better witness to them about Christ. It also makes God real and personal to us. Merely reading in the Bible about God's love is not enough. Seek to *experience* that love in your heart by sharing it with others.

Just as truth is victorious over lies (vv. 1–6), love is victorious over fear (vv. 17–19). As you mature in your love for God, you realize that you have nothing to fear, for your Father has everything under control. You trust those you love, and faith and love will give victory over fear.

1 JOHN 5

When you are born of God, you are born to love (vv. 1–3). You will love the Father who gave you life and the Son who gave His life for you. You will also love His children, for you all belong to the same family.

When you are born of God, you are born to win (vv. 4–5). Your first birth made you a sinner and a loser, but your second birth makes you a conqueror. The world wants to entice you (2:15–17) and the devil wants to seduce you (Gen. 3:6), but Christ will give you the victory you need if you trust Him.

When you are born of God, you are born to assurance (vv. 6–13), and you can know that you have eternal life. You are also born to talk to your Father in prayer and receive from Him what you need (vv. 14–17).

When you are born of God, you are born secure, and the evil one cannot harm you (vv. 18–21). You do not keep yourself saved, for the Father does that (John 10:27–30); but you keep yourself from the clutches of the wicked one. As you abide in Christ, you experience His love and care.

SECOND JOHN

◆

John wrote this letter to an anonymous Christian woman whose home was open for God's people to meet for fellowship and worship. The emphasis is on truth and love, and John points out three dangers believers must avoid.

Knowing the truth but not practicing it (1–6). We must walk in truth and walk according to His commandments. The Word of God is meant for *doing* and not just *knowing.* "If we say" (1 John 1:6, 8, 10) but do not obey, we are hypocrites.

Practicing truth but not defending it (7–8, 10–11). The enemy is busy, and we must oppose him. Love must be balanced by truth (Eph. 4:15), or you will start supporting lies in the name of love (Phil. 1:9–11). It is easy to lose what you have gained by making friends with the wrong people.

Going beyond the truth (9). The word *transgress* means "to go beyond." When you go beyond God's Word, you are going too far. It is not progress but regress. Beware anybody who has something to add to your Bible.

❝Truth is always strong, no matter how weak it looks,
and falsehood is always weak, no matter
how strong it looks.**❞**

Phillips Brooks

THIRD JOHN

———————◆———————

John wrote this letter to his friend Gaius to encourage him in a difficult situation in his local church. Again, he concentrated on making God's truth a vital part of life.

Walking in truth (1–4). People could see the truth in Gaius because he loved it and walked in obedience to it, and that brought great joy to John. Every Christian parent can echo verse 4 and even make it a prayer.

Working for truth (5–8). When you assist and encourage God's servants, you become a fellow worker with them in spreading the truth. Christian hospitality was important in those days and ought to be revived today.

Welcoming the truth (9–10). Can you imagine Diotrephes rejecting a message from the apostle John! He was so "separated" that he did not even receive John's friends. When we welcome God's people, we welcome God's truth.

Witnessing for the truth (11–14). Not all church members are like Diotrephes; there are people like Demetrius who love the truth and live it. They are the ones who make the local church healthy (v. 2).

JUDE

Jude, like James, was a half brother of the Lord Jesus (Mark 6:3). His letter focuses on false teachers and echoes Peter's warnings in 2 Peter 2.

Who they are (1–4). Jude wanted to write about salvation, but the Lord directed him to write about invasion instead. False teachers were creeping into the church and going undetected. These are unsaved people (v. 19), ungodly people, and unprincipled people who use grace as an excuse for sin.

Seek Wisdom	In trying to minister to people, we must be careful and exercise discernment lest they do us more harm than we do good (Jude 22–23). Concerning the Pharisees, Jesus said to His disciples, "Let them alone" (Matt. 15:14). God told the prophet Hosea, "Ephraim is joined to idols, let him alone" (Hos. 4:17). And Paul told Timothy to withdraw himself from certain troublemakers (1 Tim. 6:3–5). Ask God for wisdom as you seek to help persons wandering from the faith.

What they do (5–11). Like the Jews in the wilderness, the fallen angels, and the evil cities of the plain, they reject the authority of God. Their words are defiant and defiling. Like Cain (Gen. 4), they have no saving faith, but they do have reli-

gion. Like Balaam (Num. 22—24), they use religion as a way to make money; and like Korah (Num. 16), they defy the Word of God and the authority of God's chosen servants.

What they are (12–16). False teachers promise much but produce little, like rainless clouds and fruitless trees. Enoch had the best word for them: *ungodly.*

What we must do (17–25). Remember the Word and build yourself up in your Christian faith. True believers are "preserved in Jesus Christ" (v. 1), and they prove this by keeping themselves in God's love (v. 21). Therefore, God can keep them from falling (vv. 24–25).

THE REVELATION OF JESUS CHRIST

---◆---

John was a Roman prisoner on the Isle of Patmos when God gave him this revelation of Jesus Christ. The book reveals Jesus Christ the Priest-King (chap. 1), the Judge of the churches (chaps. 2—3), the Creator (chap. 4), the Redeemer (chap. 5), the Lord of history (chaps. 6—18), the Conqueror (chaps. 19—20), and the Bridegroom (chaps. 21—22). The key name for Christ in this book is *the Lamb*. John never lets you forget that Jesus died for the sins of the world (John 1:29).

Another key word is *throne,* used over forty times. The Revelation describes the conflict between the throne of the Lamb in heaven and the throne of Satan on earth. As John writes, he depicts worship in heaven and warfare on earth; and the Lord is the victor. No matter how dark the day or how strong the forces of evil, the Lamb of God wins the victory.

The key verse is 1:19. John is told to write "the things which you have seen [chap. 1], and the things which are [chaps. 2—3], and the things which will take place after this [chaps. 4—22]."

Revelation 6—19 parallels Matthew 24 and Mark 13 in describing the day of the Lord or the Tribulation. The first part is described in chapters 6—9; the middle in chapters 10—14; and the last part ("the great tribulation") in chapters 15—19. While good and godly people disagree on the details of interpreting John's numbers and symbols, most agree that the last days will be marked by the increase of evil, the rise of a world government and world ruler, the attempt of Satan to destroy God's people, the pouring out of God's wrath on a rebellious world, and the return of Jesus Christ to deliver His own and establish His kingdom.

As you read, do not get lost in details, but try to see the big picture. And keep in mind that John wrote this book to encourage believers who were going through persecution. Every generation of Christians has had its Antichrist and Babylon, and the hope of the Lord's return has kept the saints going when the going was tough.

Revelation is the climax of the Bible, the fulfillment of what God started in Genesis. Many symbols in Genesis are found in this fascinating book: light and darkness, stars, Babylon, the bride, a garden, a tree of life, a serpent, and so on. He is "the Alpha and the Omega" (1:8). What He starts, He finishes.

REVELATION 1

This book is first of all the revelation of Jesus Christ, not just the revelation of future events. Before John describes endtime events, he describes the Lord Jesus and reminds you of who He is and what He has done.

A Blessed Book	*You will find seven "beatitudes" in Revelation: 1:3; 14:13; 16:15; 19:9; 20:6; 22:7, 14. It is indeed a book with a blessing!*

Let Your Light Shine	*In the Old Testament tabernacle, there was one lampstand with seven branches; but here John saw seven lampstands (Rev. 1:12), symbolizing the seven churches addressed in chapters 2—3 (v. 20). Each local assembly of believers should shine for the Lord (Matt. 5:16) by holding fast the Word of life and proclaiming it in a dark world (Phil. 2:14–16).*

According to verse 5, He is the faithful witness (the Prophet), the firstborn from the dead (the Priest), and the ruler over the kings of the earth (the King). He is also the Savior (vv. 5b–6) who has made His people a kingdom of priests (Exod. 19:1–6; 1 Pet. 2:1–10). Never forget that Jesus shed His blood for you, and that His blood cleanses (1:5; 7:14), redeems (5:9), and overcomes (12:11).

When John was in the Upper Room, he leaned on Jesus' bosom (John 13:23); but when he saw the glorified Christ, he fell at His feet as a dead man (v. 17; 2 Cor. 5:16). Like John, we must begin with worship if God's revelations in this book are to have any meaning to us.

One day "there shall be no more death" (21:4) because Jesus has conquered death (v. 18). When you know Him as Savior and Lord, you need not fear the future; He has the keys in His hand.

REVELATION 2—3

Judgment begins at "the house of God" (1 Pet. 4:17), so Jesus deals with the seven churches before He deals with the lost world. These churches illustrate the good and the bad in churches everywhere and in every age. If you were looking for a church to join, which of these seven would you select and why?

Ephesus (2:1–7). There is so much good in this church that we are surprised to discover they had left (not lost) their first love. The honeymoon was over (Jer. 2:2)! No amount of separation, sacrifice, or service can make up for your lack of love toward the Lord. The word *Nicolaitans* means "conquer the people." Apparently a group in the church lorded it over the people and promoted a separation of "clergy" and "laity." (See Matt. 21:20–27; 23:1–12.)

Smyrna (2:8–11). The name *Smyrna* comes from "myrrh," which is a bitter herb, a suitable name for a church facing persecution. Would the believers be *fearful* or *faithful* (v. 10)? Suffering can enrich us, even if we think we are poor; and what people think is wealth might turn out to be poverty (3:17)! What difference does it make if people slander you so long as you have the Lord's approval?

Pergamos (2:12–17). These believers held to the faith even

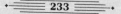

when it might have cost them their lives. But they were too tolerant of false doctrine and were in danger of having the Lord declare war on the church. Balaam convinced Israel to compromise with their unbelieving neighbors, disobey the Lord, and indulge in immorality (Num. 22—24). Being willing to die for the faith is no substitute for living the faith.

Thyatira (2:18—29). Verse 19 gives you the impression that all is well in the church, but keep reading! Like the saints in Pergamos, the believers in Thyatira tolerated sin in the church. Idolatry and immorality usually go together, and Jezebel personifies both (1 Kings 16:29–34; 21; 2 Kings 9:30–37). Not everybody in the fellowship was guilty of sin, and the Lord did not warn them. Instead, He encouraged them to hold to the truth and be faithful.

Sardis (3:1—6). This church had a great reputation, but close examination showed that its ministry did not live up to its name. In fact, the church was ready to die! What was the cause? Many of the people were defiling themselves by compromising with sin (2 Cor. 6:14–18; James 1:27). The "Book of Life" contains the names of all living persons; and when a person dies without Christ, the name is blotted out. Believers have their names in the Lamb's Book of Life and can never be blotted out.

Philadelphia (3:7—13). The name means "brotherly love," and Jesus had a special love for these people (v. 9). Weak as they were, they were given an open door of service; and the Lord urged them to take advantage of it. When God opens a door for you, nobody can shut it; but you can ignore or neglect it.

Laodicea (3:14—22). This church did not know how bad off it was! It was a working church, but its service was lukewarm. The members lacked spiritual enthusiasm. It was a wealthy church, but it was really poor—and did not know its own sad condition. Worst of all, the Lord was *outside the church trying to get in!* If only one member would yield to Him, the church could be changed.

God's people must be open and honest with the Lord and humbly submit to His spiritual diagnosis. No church or Christian is so far gone that He cannot bring renewal, but we must be willing to repent and return to Him.

To the Overcomers

Each of these messages to the churches ends with a promise to the overcomers. These overcomers are not an elite group in the church but true believers who have trusted Christ (1 John 5:1–5). No matter how unspiritual an assembly may become, Christ will always honor those who belong to Him if they are faithful to His Word. The promises to the overcomers follow Old Testament history, from the Garden of Eden (Rev. 2:7) to the kingdom throne (3:21).

REVELATION 4

A door (1). God will one day open the door, the trumpet will sound, and God's people will be called to heaven (1 Thess. 4:13–18). Meanwhile, we must take advantage of the open door of service that He gives us (3:8).

A throne (2, 4–5). Revelation is the book of the throne. John saw God the Father on the throne and was so overwhelmed that he had to refer to precious stones to describe what he beheld. Satan may have his throne on earth (2:13), but God's throne in heaven rules over all and will not be defeated.

A rainbow (3). This emerald rainbow was *around* the throne, a complete circle and not just an arc. It pictures the grace of God (Gen. 9:11–17). On earth, we see the rainbow *after* the storm; but John saw it *before* the storm of judgment came. God gives His people His gracious promise, and they need not fear the coming storm (3:10; 1 Thess. 1:10; 5:8).

A choir (6–11). The living creatures represent creation praising the Creator (Gen. 1:26–31), and the elders represent God's people worshiping Him. When you lose the wonder of the Creator, you cease to become a good steward of the creation (11:18). All of creation praises the Lord while sinful man praises himself and ignores his Creator.

> *"The more I study nature, the more I am amazed at the Creator."*
>
> Louis Pasteur

> *"Thus does the world forget You, its Creator, and falls in love with what You have created instead of with You."*
>
> Augustine

REVELATION 5

The scroll (1) represents the title deed to creation, for Jesus Christ alone is the rightful Heir (Ps. 2:8; Heb. 1:2). Satan offered Him the whole world in return for one act of worship (Matt. 4:8–10), but Jesus won the right to receive the scroll when He gave Himself on the cross. Have you placed the scroll of your life in His hands?

The Lamb (5–6) is Jesus Christ who was slain as a sacrifice for sin (1 Pet. 1:18–20); He is both Lamb (John 1:29) and Lion (Gen. 49:8–10), the Savior and the Sovereign. He is also the Root of David, for He existed before David and brought David's kingly line into being. As Lamb, Jesus offers salvation; as Lion, He judges those who reject Him. Marvel at the many aspects of His person and work!

The incense (8) represents prayer (Ps. 141:1–3). For centuries, God's people have been praying, "Thy kingdom come"; and those prayers are about to be answered. Saints on earth do not pray to or through the saints now in heaven; our praying is to the Father and through the Son. But the prayers of God's people play a vital part in God's governing of the world.

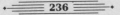

The worship (9–14). He is worthy of our worship, not only because He is Creator (chap. 4) but even more because He is our Redeemer. See how the circle of praise grows until every creature worships Him. Heaven is a place of worship, so begin to get ready now to join in the praise!

"*If the veil of the world's machinery were lifted off, how much we would find is done in answer to the prayers of God's children.***"**

Robert Murray M'Cheyne

REVELATION 6

The world ruler (Antichrist) begins his conquest of the nations by peacefully taking control (vv. 1–2). He has a weapon but no ammunition; and men are saying, "Peace and safety!" (1 Thess. 5:1–3). Satan usually declares peace before he declares war, so beware his offers.

Counterfeit Christ

There are two important riders in Revelation: Antichrist at the opening of the book (6:1–2) and Christ at the close (19:11–16). The prefix *anti* in Greek means "instead of" as well as "against." The world ruler is a counterfeit Christ, energized by the master counterfeiter, Satan (2 Cor. 11:13–15). John does not use the term Antichrist; instead, he calls him "the beast" (chap. 13). The world would not receive the true Christ, but it will receive the false Christ (John 5:43).

Soon the world is at war (vv. 3-4), and suffering results from famine and plagues (vv. 5-8) and cosmic disturbances (vv. 12-17). Jesus said these things would happen (Matt. 24:4-13).

The martyrs are seen "under the altar" because that is where the blood was placed (Lev. 4:7; 17:11). Death for Jesus' sake is not waste; it is sacrifice and worship. They pray not for personal vengeance but for God's glorification and vindication. When it appears that God is not working as you think He should, be patient and let Him do His will in His time.

> **❝**Love makes the whole difference between
> an execution and a martyrdom.**❞**
>
> Evelyn Underhill

REVELATION 7

When the storm starts to get worse, John sees two groups of people and takes courage. Why? Because he realizes that God is at work even in the midst of tribulation.

God has His servants who will proclaim His message and honor His name (vv. 1-8). We are not told what these sealed Jews will do, but we assume they will point people to the Lord. Times of tribulation give opportunities for witness (Matt. 24:14).

> **❝**We make a great mistake if we connect with our
> conception of heaven the thought of rest from work.
> Rest from toil, from weariness, from exhaustion—yes;
> rest from work, from productiveness, from service—
> no. 'They serve God day and night.'**❞**
>
> B. F. Westcott

Apparently the 144,000 Jews will be sealed at the beginning of the Tribulation; and at the end, a great multitude of saved Gentiles will be seen (vv. 9–17). The day of the Lord will bring judgment and destruction, and it will also result in the saving of people. In wrath, God remembers mercy (Hab. 3:2). When you experience trials, ask God to use you to win others to the Savior even in the midst of troubles.

Trials do not last forever. One day, you will come out of tribulation and experience the gracious comforts of God. Wait and be faithful, and He will see you through.

REVELATION 8—9

Incense at the altar (8:1–4). The silence in heaven is the lull before the storm (Hab. 2:20; Zeph. 1:7). Even the heavenly hosts stop their worship as they contemplate the awesome judgments about to fall. But those judgments are the answer to the saints' prayers (5:8), "Thy kingdom come!" Do not stop praying!

Fire from the altar (8:5—9:12). The world will not come to the altar for forgiveness (9:21), so the altar sends forth judgment. Heaven and earth are struck as the trumpets sound, and the bottomless pit belches out demonic creatures to torment mankind. Rather than repent, people will try to commit suicide; but they will not be able to die (9:6). They will continue in their sins: occult practices, murder, immorality, and thievery (9:20–21), all of which sound very contemporary.

A voice from the altar (9:13–21). God has His legions ready to be released at the right time, and torment will be replaced by death. Men have wanted to die, so God will send His servants to do the job. One-third of mankind will be killed (9:15), which means that half of the world's population is now dead (6:8)! The world must make a choice: life or death (Deut. 30:19). Are you offering them the gift of life in Jesus Christ?

REVELATION 10

The voice of the thunders (1–4). We do not know what the angel shouted or what the seven thunders uttered (Ps. 29). God has given sufficient truth in His Word for salvation and godly living, so we must not crave to know the hidden things (Deut.

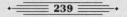

29:29). The purpose of Scripture is to save sinners and sanctify character, not satisfy curiosity.

The voice of the angel (5–7). The angel said, "There will be delay no longer!" What joy this statement will bring to the martyrs (and others) who ask, "How long?" (6:9–11). God has His times (Eccles. 3:1–8) and will accomplish His purposes on schedule. Our responsibility is to be faithful and not inquisitive (Acts 1:6–8).

The voice of the apostle (8–11). God still needed John to declare His message to the people. No angel could take his place. But to share God's message, we must take the Word, receive it inwardly like food, and let it become part of us (Jer. 15:16; Ezek. 3:1–11; 1 Thess. 2:13). The Word is sweet when you read it (Ps. 119:103) but bitter when it goes deeper and you digest it.

"If you conscientiously undertake to walk in the truth revealed, you too will know something of its bitterness. . . . We need the bitter as well as the sweet; and every soul who has walked in the truth, as God has revealed it to him, has found, at last, the blessedness of obedience."

H. A. Ironside

REVELATION 11

To measure something is to claim it for yourself, as when the new owner of a house measures it for carpets, drapes, and so forth. John claims the temple in Jerusalem for the Lord even though in a short time the Antichrist will take it over (2 Thess. 2:3–4). God may seem to lose some battles, but He will finally win the war. We walk by faith.

We do not know who the two witnesses are, but they encourage us to be faithful to the Lord in difficult times. God

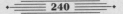

protects them and then permits them to be slain (Acts 12:1–10). God's servants are immortal until their work is done. But Satan's victory is short, for God takes the two men to heaven. Satan's victory is defeat, but God's seeming defeat is victory.

No matter what the enemy may do to the temple on earth, he cannot touch the temple in heaven (v. 19). The rejoicing of evil men soon becomes lamentation (vv. 10–14), while the hosts of heaven proclaim the sovereign reign of Jesus Christ (vv. 15–18). Let the nations rage (Ps. 2): Jesus Christ will reign forever and ever!

“*No doctrine in the whole Word of God has more excited the hatred of mankind than the truth of the absolute sovereignty of God. The fact that ‘the Lord reigneth’ is indisputable, and it is this fact that arouses the utmost opposition in the unrenewed human heart.***”**

Charles Haddon Spurgeon

REVELATION 12

The Murderer (1–6). The Child is Jesus Christ, and the woman represents Israel who brought the Savior into the world. The dragon is Satan who tried to keep Jesus from being born and attempted to kill Him after He was born. Satan wants to rule this world, and he will not submit to the King (v. 5; Ps. 2:9).

The Deceiver (7–9). This is a picture of the fall of Satan (Isa. 14:12–17). He was able to deceive one-third of the angels into following him (v. 4), and now he deceives the world into worshiping him.

The Accuser (10–12). Satan has access to God's throne where he accuses God's people (Job 1—2; Zech. 3). The Lamb overcomes him because of His victory at Calvary (Rom. 8:31–34; 1 John 2:1–2) and because of the power of the Word (Eph. 6:17).

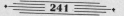

The Persecutor (13–17). The war may be over in heaven, but it it getting more intense here on earth. Satan is angry and seeks to destroy the Jews and make war with anyone who trusts the Lord. God is able to shelter His people in spite of Satan's attacks, but be sure you wear the armor (Eph. 6:10–18) and trust the blood of Jesus.

❝I'm not afraid of the devil. The devil can handle me—he's got judo I never heard of. But he can't handle the One to whom I'm joined; he can't handle the One to whom I'm united; he can't handle the One whose nature dwells in my nature.**❞**

A. W. Tozer

REVELATION 13

Worship. The beast from the sea is Satan's final and greatest masterpiece—Antichrist, who towers above all the tyrants and dictators of world history. This man accepts the offer that Satan gave to Jesus (v. 2; Matt. 4:8–10). The world worships him as a god, but heaven sees him as a beast (Dan. 7). The counterfeit Christ is now on the scene!

Warfare. The Beast fights God by speaking blasphemous words (Dan. 7:8, 11, 20, 25) and by persecuting the saints (v. 7; Dan. 7:25). It may seem strange that God should permit His people to be defeated, yet this is part of His plan (Heb. 11:35–40). In every age, God's people have had to battle some satanic beast.

Wealth. The Beast's "prime minister" leads the world to worship the Beast by controlling all the wealth. It was a matter of life or death! When you combine political power with economic power and all religion, you have a formula for controlling the whole world. But the lost world worships money and power, so the task will not be too difficult.

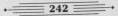

Which Riches Are Yours

Since all the riches of this world
May be gifts from the Devil and earthly kings,
I should suspect that I worshiped the Devil
If I thanked God for worldly things.
The countless gold of a merry heart,
The rubies and pearls of a loving eye,
The indolent never can bring to the mart,
Nor the cunning hoard up in his treasury.

William Blake

REVELATION 14

John used agricultural images to tell us that the time was ripe for judgment.

Firstfruits (1–5). God takes the best for Himself before the harvest begins. We met the 144,000 in chapter 7, God's sealed servants who come through the Tribulation and sing the praises of the Lamb. The description in verse 4 should be taken in a spiritual sense: they did not commit fornication by worshiping the Beast or his image (Exod. 34:15; James 4:4).

Wine (6–13). The "cup of wrath" is an image borrowed from Jeremiah 25:15ff. God pours out His wrath on those who follow the Beast and reject God's truth. Although verse 13 may be applied to all believers who die, it will have a special meaning to the martyrs of that evil day.

Reaping (14–20). God is allowing the seeds of sin to grow and produce a harvest (vv. 14–16). One day, the world will reap what it has sown. John also uses the grape harvest to illustrate the coming judgment (vv. 17–20). The "vine of the earth" is ripening, and one day God will apply the sickle. Meanwhile, the branches in the True Vine (John 15:1–8) should be bearing more and more fruit.

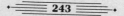

REVELATION 15

John reaches back into the Old Testament to teach us about God's judgment and grace. The seven angels have bowls of wrath, plagues to pour on a wicked world. They remind us of the plagues God sent to Egypt in the days of Moses (Exod. 7—12). Note in chapter 16 how the plagues parallel those God sent to Egypt.

God delivered Israel from Egypt, and they sang a song of victory at the Red Sea (Exod. 15). John saw the tribulation victors singing by the heavenly sea of glass. Moses and the Lamb come together in the song of triumph.

The heavenly tabernacle is filled with smoke, just as the glory of God filled both the tabernacle (Exod. 40:34-38) and the temple (1 Kings 8:10-11). But the glory then was a mark of God's presence and blessing. The glory John saw was an announcement that God's wrath was about to be poured out on a wicked world.

Sinners will not learn from the past, but believers can be encouraged by the past. The God of Moses and Israel is still defending His people. There is a new song for you to sing.

REVELATION 16

No matter what the unbelieving world may say, God's judgments are righteous (vv. 1–7). Sinners reap what they sow. Because "righteousness and justice are the foundation of His throne" (Ps. 97:2), nobody can accuse God of being unfair.

God's judgments do not change men's hearts (vv. 8–11). God judges sinners not to reveal His grace but to uphold His holiness. Sinners in the last days will be like Pharaoh in the days of Moses; they will harden their hearts more as God's judgments increase.

Against the dark background of judgment shines the promise of God (vv. 12–16). Christ is coming soon, and we must watch eagerly and walk carefully (3:1-6) so that we will be ready to meet Him (1 John 2:28).

God's judgment will one day be finished (vv. 17–21). God's long-suffering will finally end, and His wrath will be revealed. What holds Him back today? Read 2 Peter 3:9, 15 for the answer.

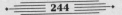

> *In righteousness God reveals chiefly His love of holiness; in justice, chiefly his hatred of sin . . . Neither justice nor righteousness . . . is a matter of arbitrary will. They are revelations of the inmost nature of God.*

Augustus Hopkins Strong

The Battlefield

Armageddon (*Rev. 16:16*) is Hebrew for "the hill of Megiddo"; and Megiddo means "place of slaughter." It is the plain in the Holy Land where Barak defeated the Canaanites (*Judg. 5:19*) and Gideon the Midianites (*Judg. 7*). King Saul fought his last battle there (*1 Sam. 31*). One of the greatest natural battlefields in the world, it is where the Antichrist will gather the world's armies to fight against Jesus Christ (*Isa. 24; Joel 3; Zech. 12—14*). Revelation 19:11–21 records the outcome.

REVELATION 17

Each person must identify with either the harlot or the bride (21:9); there can be no compromise. The woman represents the ultimate in godless world religion. She is joined with government (carried by the Beast) and corrupts everything she touches. The bride is the true church of Jesus Christ, cleansed by His blood and destined for glory.

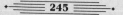

Participating in false religion is like committing adultery: you are unfaithful to the one to whom you pledged your love (Isa. 57:3; Jer. 3:8–9; Hos. 2:4). The harlot was popular for a time, but then her "lovers" turned on her and destroyed her. The Antichrist will use a world church to get himself into power and then establish his own religion (13:11–15).

Though Christians must be good citizens and seek to influence government for the Lord, the church must not marry political systems. The systems will only use the church to promote their own plans and then abandon it. Christ's kingdom is not of this world (John 18:33–38), and the enemy is spiritual (Eph. 6:10ff.). We must use spiritual weapons (2 Cor. 10:3–6) to fight spiritual enemies.

REVELATION 18

The harlot and the bride are each identified with a city: the harlot with Babylon and the bride with heavenly Jerusalem (21:9ff.). The heavenly city will be the bride's home for eternity, but Babylon will be destroyed by God. The world's economy will be ruined.

❝In our well-intentioned identification with the world, we do not mold it—it molds us. We are not to be isolated but insulated, moving in the midst of evil but untouched by it.**❞**

Vance Havner

John certainly had Rome in mind when he wrote this chapter, but his imagery means much more. Babylon symbolizes the whole godless world system that caters to the appetites of sinful men and women (1 John 2:15–17). True believers have nothing in common with the harlot and her city and should be separated from them (v. 4; Jer. 50:8; 51:6; 2 Cor. 6:14–18). In every age, the church has had to identify its Babylon and separate from it.

When God judges sinners, earth laments and heaven rejoices (v. 20). Most people are concerned primarily with satisfying their physical desires; they are not concerned about things spiritual or eternal. They live for the temporary and the immediate, not the eternal.

REVELATION 19

Celebration (1–6). Sinners cry "Alas!" but saints shout "Hallelujah!" at the fall of the godless world system called Babylon. Sin has been judged, God's servants have been vindicated, God has been glorified, and Christ is about to usher in His kingdom. Even as you anticipate these victories, by faith you can shout "Hallelujah!"

Proclamation (7–10, 17–21). Two contrasting suppers are named in this chapter: the marriage supper of the Lamb (v. 9), which brings blessing, and the "supper of the great God" (vv. 17–21), which brings judgment. The bride makes herself ready at the judgment seat of Christ where her "spots and wrinkles" are taken away (Eph. 5:25–27) and she receives rewards for faithful service. In contrast, the godless armies of earth are defeated by the Lord and become food for the birds. This is the battle of Armageddon mentioned in Revelation 16:16.

The Coming Kingdom

His kingdom is coming!
Oh, tell me the story!
God's banner exalted shall be;
The earth shall be filled with His wonder and glory,
As waters that cover the sea.

Anonymous

Revelation (11–16). The conquering Christ comes with His armies and defeats all His enemies! Contrast this with His ride into Jerusalem on Palm Sunday (Matt. 21:1–11), and review the Father's promises in Psalm 2. Also contrast it with the ride of the Antichrist (6:1–2). It encourages us to know that our Savior is *today* King of kings and Lord of lords, and that the future is secure because He is reigning.

REVELATION 20

The lost throne (1–3, 7–10). Since Satan's rebellion (Isa. 14:12–15), God has permitted him to work on this earth, but He has always kept him in control (Job 1—2). Satan will exchange his throne for a bottomless pit, and his final destiny will be the lake of fire where he will spend eternity with the Beast and the false prophet (v. 10; 19:20)—and with those who choose to follow Satan instead of Jesus Christ (Matt. 25:41).

The kingdom thrones (4–6). The first resurrection takes place before Jesus ushers in His kingdom and involves only those who have trusted Christ (John 5:24–29; 1 Thess. 4:13–18). They will reign with Him (Matt. 19:28) and have responsibilities commensurate with their faithful service while living on earth (Matt. 25:14–30).

The great white throne (11–15). This judgment involves only the lost and follows the second resurrection, the resurrection to condemnation. Sinners who rejected Christ will face Him (John 5:22) and hear Him say, "Depart from Me!" (Matt. 7:23; 25:41). This solemn scene ought to move us to pray for the lost and witness to them, and thank the Lord for His grace in saving us!

REVELATION 21

For those who believe in Jesus Christ, the future means "all things new" (v. 5); but for those who reject Him, it means the same old sins for all eternity (vv. 8, 27; 22:11, 15).

Human history begins with a garden (Gen. 2:8–17) and ends with a city that is like a garden. However, the most important thing about the heavenly city is not the absence of sin but the presence of God in all His glory (vv. 3, 11, 23), for His presence makes "all things new."

He is the temple (v. 22) and the light (v. 23); and His presence means there is no more sin, pain, death, sorrow, or crying (v. 4), and no more curse (22:3; Gen. 3:9–19). Heaven is so wonderful that the only way John can describe it is to tell us what will *not* be there! Its beauties and blessings are beyond human words to describe or explain.

Why did Jesus give John this preview of eternal glory? *To encourage His people who go through testing and persecution.* "I go to prepare a place for you" (John 14:1–6) is the best medicine for a broken heart and the best foundation for wavering feet.

> **❝***The hope of heaven under troubles is like the wind and sails to the soul.***❞**
>
> Samuel Rutherford

> **❝***No man ought to look for anything in heaven but what one way or another he has some experience in this life.***❞**
>
> John Owen

REVELATION 22

How do you respond to the promise of the Lord's return? John's last chapter can help you take inventory.

Are you treasuring His Word and obeying it (v. 7)? This is *His* message to you (v. 16), and it must not be altered (vv. 18–19). There is a special blessing for the obedient (v. 14).

Are you doing the work He has called you to do (v. 12)? He promises to reward faithful servants (Luke 12:35–48).

Do you really *want* Jesus to return today (v. 20)? Do you "love His appearing" (2 Tim. 4:8)? If Jesus were to come today, would you be disappointed and your plans be upset?

Are you urging lost sinners to trust Him and be ready for His coming (v. 17)? The Holy Spirit works through the church to bring lost people to the Savior. The people described in 21:8

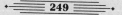

and 22:11 can be saved (1 Cor. 6:9–11) and become new creatures ready for the new heaven and earth (2 Cor. 5:17). Will you tell them?

"Amazing Grace"

Amazing grace! How sweet the sound,
That saved a wretch like me!
I once was lost, but now am found;
Was blind, but now I see!

When we've been there ten thousand years,
Bright shining as the sun,
We've no less days to sing God's praise
Than when we'd first begun.

John Newton

NOTES

NOTES

NOTES

NOTES

NOTES

NOTES